Welcome

Sixty years ago, a young Paul Simon and Art Garfunkel signed with Columbia Records, but little did they know it would be their first step on a journey to the pantheon of music history. This special edition celebrates the story of folk-rock's greatest duo, from sublime musical harmony to infamous personal discord. Discover more about Paul Simon and Art Garfunkel's early friendship, how a chance remix of 'The Sound of Silence' catapulted them to fame, and see how their sound evolved during their careers – both together and apart. Explore their critically acclaimed back catalogue with track-by-track analysis of every album, and delve into the artistic tensions that led to one of music's most renowned on-again, off-again relationships.

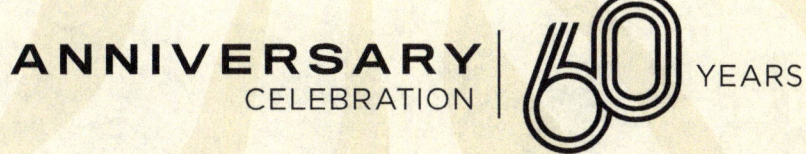

Contents

CHAPTER 1
- **8**   **When Arthur Met Paul**
- **16**   **Tom & Jerry**
- **24**   **One and Done?**

CHAPTER 2
- **30**   **The Sound of Success**
- **46**   **The Graduate Soundtrack**
- **54**   **The Beginning of the End**

CHAPTER 3
- **66**   **The Breakup**
- **72**   **Art Garfunkel**
- **82**   **Paul Simon**

CHAPTER 4
- **94**   **Reunite, Split, Repeat**
- **104**   **Simon & Garfunkel's Legacy**

Discography

- 20   WEDNESDAY MORNING, 3.A.M. (1964)
- 38   SOUNDS OF SILENCE (1966)
- 42   PARSLEY, SAGE, ROSEMARY AND THYME (1966)
- 50   BOOKENDS (1968)
- 60   BRIDGE OVER TROUBLED WATER (1970)

Chapter 1

8
WHEN ARTHUR MET PAUL

16
TOM & JERRY

20
WEDNESDAY MORNING, 3.A.M. (1964)

24
ONE AND DONE?

Before the greatest vocal duo in history hit the big time, they were just regular kids – if also unusually talented ones…

WORDS BY **JOEL McIVER**

When Arthur met Paul

The joys and the tragedies of the Paul Simon and Art Garfunkel story are both bound up in the same simple fact: that the two men were so similar – at least in their early lives – that they were drawn together and then forced apart. Educated, cultured, and of Jewish heritage, the two men could have passed as brothers had they been of more similar stature and looks; as it was, their talents were so similar that inwardly, they formed two parts of the same individual.

Paul Simon was born on 13 October 1941, in Newark, New Jersey. His Hungarian-Jewish parents were Louis and Belle Simon, and he had a younger brother, Eddie, who looks startlingly like him and who has often been mistaken for a twin. Music – and showbiz – ran in the family thanks to Louis Simon's profile as a double bass player and dance-band leader, performing under the name Lee Sims when not holding down a prominent career as a college professor.

Academia played its part too, with Louis the holder of a doctorate and Belle an elementary school teacher. By 1945, the Simons had moved to the Kew Gardens Hills district of Flushing, Queens, in New York City, where their collective talents led to prosperity.

Chapter 1

The cover image for 'My Little Town' (1975) was taken in front of Paul Simon's childhood home.

The young Paul Simon led a lifestyle which was aptly summed up in later years by Donald Fagen of Steely Dan, who admired his work. As Fagen told *Rolling Stone*, Simon's childhood was that of "a certain kind of New York Jew, almost a stereotype really, to whom music and baseball are very important. I think it has to do with the parents, [who] are either immigrants or first-generation Americans who felt like outsiders, and assimilation was the key thought – they gravitated to Black music and baseball looking for an alternative culture." Simon, hearing this description, described it as "not far from the truth".

Before music impacted on Simon's life, baseball was everything to him: he followed the New York Yankees with absolute commitment, cycling to other neighbourhoods to play baseball and its improvised variant, stickball. Louis took his sons to Yankee Stadium to see Joe DiMaggio play, with the baseball great later immortalised in the song 'Mrs Robinson', and also to concerts, which is where music came in. One day, as Simon was singing to himself in his bedroom, his father complimented him on his voice – and the path was set.

Until he was 11 years old, Simon had no idea that his future creative partner was living three blocks from his home. Arthur Garfunkel had been born on 5 November 1941 in Forest Hills, Queens, the second of three sons to Jack, a salesman, and Rose, a housewife, in the parlance of the day. A cousin was Lou Pearlman, who later formed the pop bands Backstreet Boys and NSYNC and died a convicted fraudster in 2016. The family were of Romanian-Jewish descent, and the young Garfunkel sang in synagogues as a child.

Garfunkel's parents were both singers and encouraged their son to sing, buying him a recorder so he could tape himself singing and work on improving his performance. The Righteous Brothers' 'Unchained Melody' was among the songs that influenced him greatly in his early years, as was traditional religious music: he sang for four hours straight at his bar mitzvah in 1954.

As he explained to *Relix*: "My early singing was all about great-sounding rooms, acoustics. In my neighbourhood, there was a synagogue that had a high ceiling and wooden walls – and the reverb was wonderful. And that got me into singing. The early melodies I sang were ancient, minor-key Jewish melodies. And that minor key raised a lot of goosebumps on my arms at a very young age, and I

> **"Simon had no idea that his future creative partner lived three blocks away**

The duo grew up in the Forest Hills neighbourhood in Queens, New York.

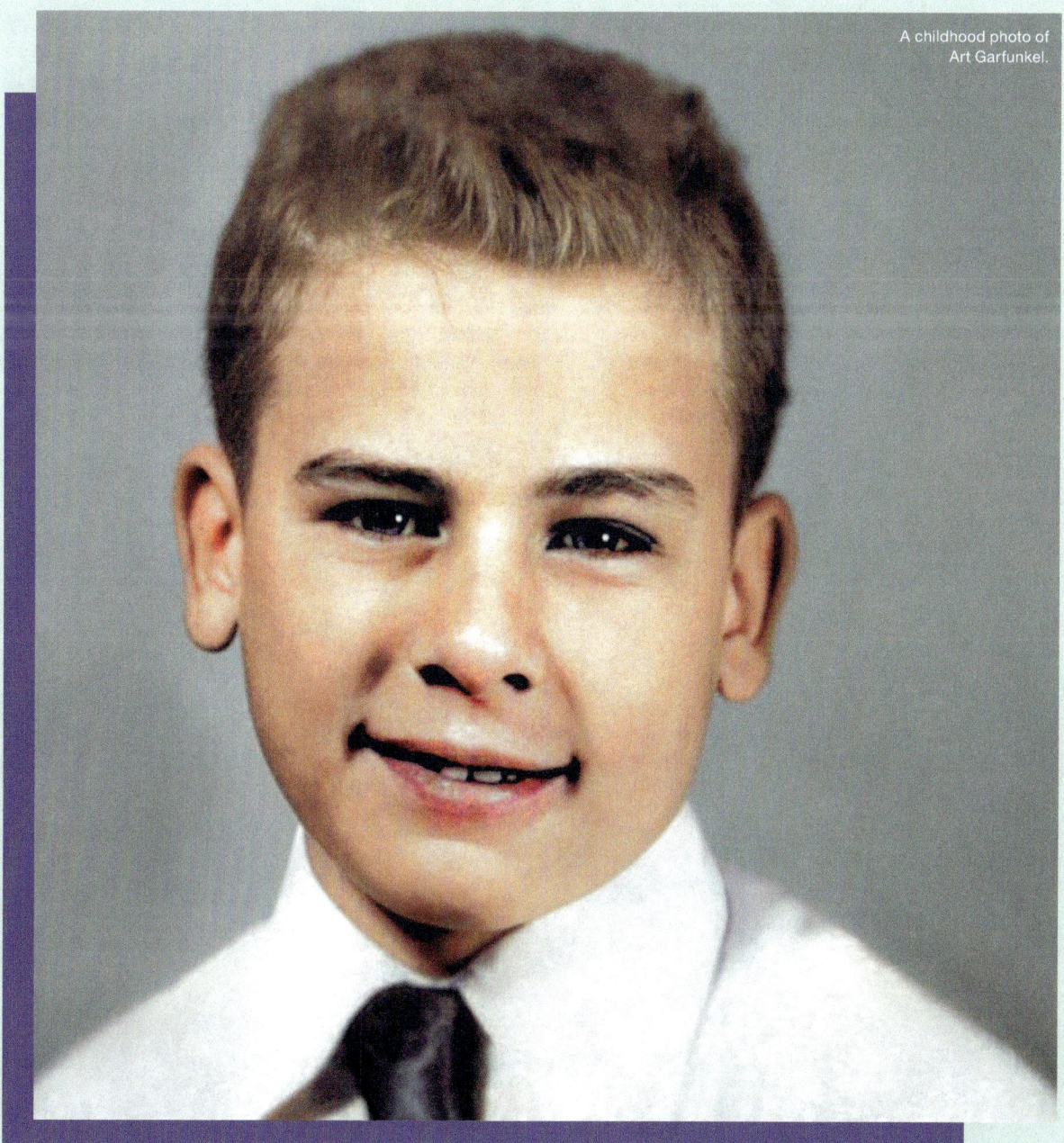

A childhood photo of Art Garfunkel.

could see it moved audiences. They'd tear up... You can call it God. You can call it whatever you want. I call it 'larger forces on Earth, that make us humble, that make us dumbstruck with the wonder of this planet'. Yes, I do the best I can to commune with these larger forces. And I sing with that kind of connection, and I hope to touch people's spirituality."

Like Simon, who he first met in 1953 during a school production of *Alice in Wonderland* in which his friend was the White Rabbit and he played the Cheshire Cat, Garfunkel soon got into sports, although by necessity rather than choice. He explained in 1998: "In the summer of '55, I had a lung infection. I couldn't run around, but I loved basketball and there was a hoop nearby. Much of the summer I spent methodically hitting 96 or 98 foul shots out of 100… I never played on a team after junior high school. Just three against three, half-court pickup games in the schoolyard."

After acting together, the two boys became friends, bonding through sports and music: they would walk home together from their school, PS 164 in Queens, and record duets on Garfunkel's tape recorder. Vocally, Simon was a little behind his synagogue-trained partner and would spend hours working on his technique, with Garfunkel making him repeat particular sounds and copy his singing style.

Chapter 1

Doo-wop was an influence on both boys at first, with Garfunkel telling *Relix*: "The Crew Cuts had a hit with 'Sh-Boom' when I was young, and that really affected me. The lead singer was up front, and the background guys were going 'Life could be a dream...' Then, the lead guy [also] goes, 'Life could be a dream'. And I heard the combination of lead and background, and it charmed me. There weren't many records when I was a kid with that. And then along came R&B. Now you have the lead singer up front and you have the rest of the group doing doo-wop. And that's another way to put the front guy ahead of the background music. I guess I was starting to see things as an arranger would in those early days."

Soul music was a motivator, too, as Simon told *Spin*: "Sam Cooke was the best voice. I don't think anybody was in Sam Cooke's league. And he also tended to be more of a soft singer and phraser, so there was more for me to learn because that's what my voice is naturally. Although he could belt too, essentially for me it was the smoothness of his voice. I was a big Sam Cooke fan, still am, even more for his work with The Soul Stirrers than for his pop stuff."

He added: "The Everly Brothers, too – [there] wouldn't have been a Simon & Garfunkel without The Everly Brothers. We sang in doo-wop groups when we were kids. We learned about singing all the three different parts, from bass to falsetto. I still do that on all my records, still put in all the background vocals myself."

A watershed moment came in 1954, as it did for millions of American kids, when Elvis Presley burst out of local radio onto national TV and into the minds of a generation. "Elvis was there. He was the most important force in rock'n'roll,

Photos of the pair from their Forest Hills High School yearbook, including a performance in the cafeteria (above).

When Arthur Met Paul

Simon and Garfunkel became friends as children, bonding over their shared love of music.

Chapter 1

no question about it," mused Simon. "Nobody even close. It was his invention, he blended Black and White music, and that's the single most powerful idea that's emerged from rock'n'roll. Plus he had the voice, a great investment."

Armed with their love of smooth doo-wop and soul, as well as beefed-up rock'n'roll, Simon and Garfunkel – yet to adopt that familiar name – continued to write songs. Simon bought a guitar and took lessons, not without some resistance: his father Louis was less than keen for his son to become a musician, especially not of the rock'n'roll kind, which was music that he despised. As for Simon's grandmother, she thought that Elvis Presley was called 'Alvin' and thus possibly Jewish; he had to let her down gently.

The budding vocal stars still had some way to go: Simon was struggling to master the guitar, given the demands of school and a part-time job he had at a children's shoe store. Still, the duo managed to complete a song called 'The Girl for Me' in 1955, copyrighting it – educated kids that they were – at the Library of Congress, Simon's father Louis having written the lyrics and chords onto music paper for them to use as reference. They performed the same year at an assembly at Parsons Junior High School, delivering a rendition of the aforementioned Crew Cuts hit 'Sh-Boom'.

At this stage, Simon and Garfunkel were essentially a tribute to The Everly Brothers, whose nasal but somehow beautiful close vocal harmonies were a significant feature of their sound. A group of fans began to coalesce around the twosome, especially after 'The Girl for Me' became – in Simon's words – a neighbourhood hit.

Gigs at school dances became regular enough for the two boys, now approaching 16, to require a name for their act. They chose to perform as Tom & Jerry, although not in reference to the popular cartoon: Simon chose the stage name Jerry Landis and Garfunkel picked Tom Graph, as he enjoyed tracking the progress of songs on the pop charts.

The turning point came when a producer called Sid Prosen offered to release one of their songs, 'Hey, Schoolgirl', on his label, Big Records. Backed with a track called 'Dancin' Wild' and released on both 45 and 78rpm vinyl, the single sold an astounding 100,000 copies throughout the US, and even charted, although at a lowly Number 49.

While these songs sound naïve and even a little primitive by the standards of the duo's later, pristine recordings, they did introduce the public to Simon and Garfunkel's most treasured asset – their unearthly vocal harmonies. The challenge that now lay before these unlikely pop-star kids was to make that early triumph into a career.

Simon and Garfunkel were both fans of the close harmonies of The Everly Brothers.

Garfunkel performed Nat King Cole's song 'Too Young' in a school talent show, which caught the attention of Simon.

Little did the young Simon and Garfunkel know, their fateful partnership would lead to huge success.

Chapter 1

The promising twosome's careers could well have finished before they began, had it not been for one song. What's that sound?

WORDS BY **DAVE SMITH**

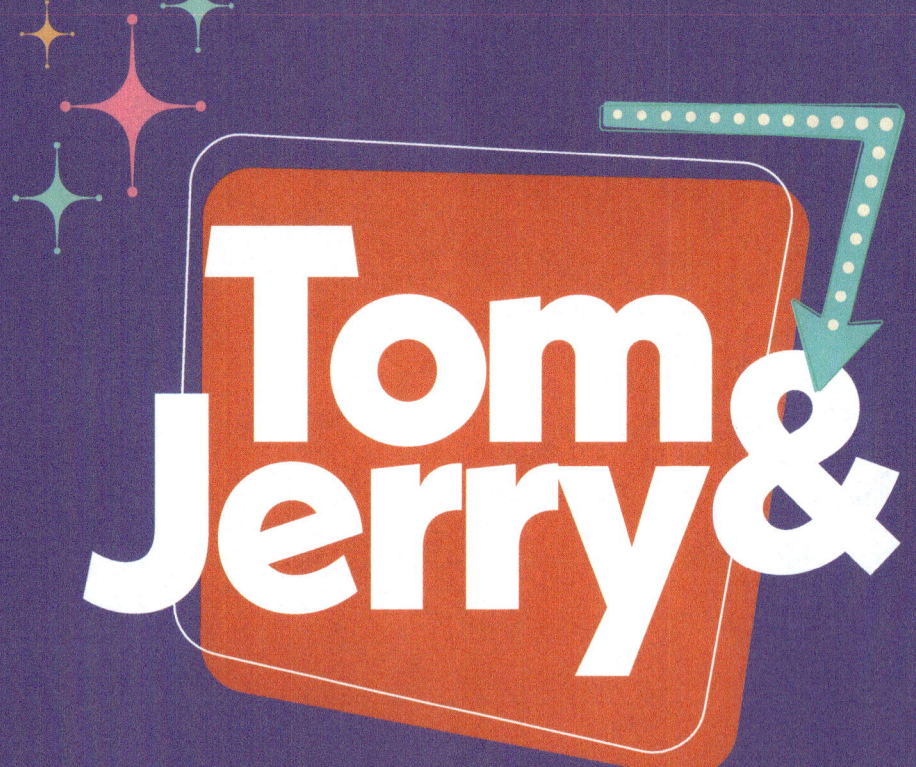

The rise of Paul Simon and Art Garfunkel seems to have been fated to take place, at least with the benefit of over six decades of hindsight – but of course it was no such thing. Talent and dedication mean nothing without luck, but fortunately for millions of fans, Paul and Art – or should we say Tom & Jerry – happened to be in the right place at exactly the right time, helped along by a little bit of bribery along the way.

What's that, you say? Yes indeed. As Paul Simon revealed many years after the fact, the pioneering rock'n'roll radio DJ Alan Freed had listened to Tom & Jerry's song 'Hey Schoolgirl' and told them that he liked it. In fact, he was prepared to play it on his show every day for two weeks, if they paid him $500, or $200 depending on which sources you consult. Somehow the duo and/or their producer Sid Prosen came up with the payola – and record sales followed.

No regrets, though. Although Freed was later busted for his payola scams and died young and partly disgraced, he was still a hero to a generation, and that generation included the young 'Tom Graph' and 'Jerry Landis'. As Garfunkel wrote in his 2017 autobiography, *What Is It All but Luminous*: "Maybe I was in the land of payola, of 'back alley enterprise' and pill-head disc jockeying, but what I felt was that Alan Freed loved us kids to dance, romance, and fall in love."

Of course, this is not meant to imply that the careers of the great folk duo were founded on dubious practices. Quite the opposite: a long period of commercial obscurity lay ahead for the two teenagers, a doldrums which they only survived through the most honest virtues possible: faith, hard work and perseverance.

To Prosen's credit, he pushed his one-hit wonders as well as he could. He swung them a slot on Dick Clark's ABC TV show *American Bandstand* alongside

Chapter 1

A portrait of Simon & Garfunkel taken in 1964 after they were signed by Columbia Records.

none other than Jerry Lee Lewis, then hot as a pistol and just as dangerous. Despite this moment in the spotlight, and the four thousand bucks which Simon and Garfunkel shared from the royalties for 'Hey Schoolgirl' – equivalent to ten times that sum in 2023 – the duo's momentum slowed and then stopped. Two more singles, 'Our Song' and 'That's My Story', were released by Prosen's Big Records label, but went nowhere: it was clearly time for Tom & Jerry to rethink their options.

Smart kids that they were, when Simon and Garfunkel graduated from Forest Hills High School in 1958, they opted to go to college, mindful that this music lark was a deeply unreliable career choice. Simon studied English at Queens College, a part of City University of New York, and Garfunkel dedicated himself to architecture before changing course to art history at Columbia University.

When music reared its head again, the two men decided to pursue their muse separately. Although the duo were still signed to Big Records, Simon adopted the stage name True Taylor and released a solo single called 'True or False': speculation has it that this irritated Garfunkel no end, perhaps even sowing the seeds of discord that would ripen decades later. In turn, he composed and recorded songs called 'Private World' and 'Beat Love' for the Octavia and Warwick record labels, the latter under the abbreviated stage name Artie Garr.

For a period of four years or so, Simon in particular was in demand as a writer and singer with other musicians: he recorded with The Mystics and Tico & The Triumphs, as well as writing his own material under the names Jerry Landis and Paul Kane. The peak of this early period of studio labour came when he worked on demo recordings with the singer-songwriter Carole King and her husband, lyricist Gerry Goffin.

In 1963, a lifetime since the old doo-wop days and the New Jersey school dances, the two crossed paths professionally once again. The Beatles were about to conquer America; Bob Dylan was on the point of redefining protest music; and Simon and Garfunkel chose to go in a folk direction, perhaps because there was nowhere else to go.

Garfunkel was still at Columbia University and Simon was pursuing part-time legal studies at Brooklyn Law School, but this didn't prevent them from performing as Kane & Garr at Gerde's Folk City, a nightclub in New York's hip Greenwich that was known for its open-mic nights on the weekly graveyard shift – Mondays.

Giving it their all with three new songs, two of which were 'Sparrow' and 'He Was My Brother', the pair impressed the visiting A&R man and Columbia Records producer Tom Wilson. He liked 'He Was My Brother' and asked the duo if he could record it with a new British act called The Pilgrims – no, us neither – but was successfully talked into letting Simon and Garfunkel audition for him at Columbia in their own right.

Come audition night, the duo sang their third new song for Wilson – which impressed him so much that he instantly instructed Columbia to offer them a deal. But which was the song that blew his mind? "Hello darkness, my old friend..."

Tom & Jerry's first single, 'Hey Schoolgirl', got to No.49 in the *Billboard* charts.

> **Despite this moment in the spotlight, the duo's momentum slowed and then stopped**

Simon and Garfunkel picked their early stage names of Jerry Landis (the surname of a girl Simon dated) and Tom Graph (as Garfunkel enjoyed maths).

Discography

WEDNESDAY MORNING, 3 A.M.

Released 19 October 1964
Words by Neil Crossley

Released amid the onset of Beatlemania, the duo's debut album was an outmoded, commercial disaster, yet it was blessed with a few real gems

You Can Tell The World
Recorded over three sessions in March 1964, *Wednesday Morning, 3 A.M.* sounds distinctly different from the classic Simon & Garfunkel duo that would emerge. This is amply demonstrated on the opening track, an effusive rendition of Bob Gibson and Bob Camp's gospel/folk song, which was first released by The Tarriers in 1960. Simon & Garfunkel's harmonising technique came straight out of The Everly Brothers, as did the slap-back echo on the vocals here. Paul and Artie were by now firmly entranced by the folk revival and there's a real unbridled, skiffle feel to this track with some gritty vocal performances.

Last Night I Had the Strangest Dream
Written by Ed McCurdy in 1950, this song was already a staple in the repertoires of the US folk community by the time Simon & Garfunkel came to record it. Joan Baez, Pete Seeger and The Kingston Trio were among those who had committed it to vinyl and it would go on to be recorded by Johnny Cash and be translated into almost 80 languages. Written during the onset of the Korean War, the composition remains one of most influential anti-war songs. Here, Simon plays banjo, alongside Barry Kornfield on acoustic guitar and Bill Lee on double bass. It's a wistful, heartfelt rendition in waltz time. Garfunkel takes the top line melody and there's an earthy texture to the duo's harmonies. The lyrics are simple and infused with idyllic hope: "I dreamed the world had all agreed / To put an end to war / I dreamed I saw a mighty room /

Tom Wilson produced some of the most famous records of the Sixties.

The room was filled with men / And the paper they were signing said / They'd never fight again."

Bleecker Street
Tom Wilson, the influential Columbia Records A&R who had signed the duo and who produced this album, insisted that the record comprised six covers and six originals. This is the first original song on the album and one of Simon's finest melancholic odes to his native city. As folk purists know, Bleecker Street is the New York thoroughfare that runs through Greenwich Village and where the duo would often play to packed houses at venues such as The Bitter End. The song features some beautifully intricate guitar work and is rich in lyrical symbolism: "Fog's rollin' off the East River Bank / Like a shroud it covers Bleecker Street / Fills the alleys where men sleep / Hides the shepherd from the sheep." This track ushers in the delicate, finely honed vocal sound that would define their careers going forward. It's a haunting ballad and one of their most overlooked gems.

Sparrow
There are strong Spanish flourishes to this delicate composition, the second Simon-penned track on the album. Lyrically, it's an allegorical tale in which the eponymous sparrow of the title

Wednesday Morning, 3 A.M.

Despite 'The Sound of Silence' being featured on this album, it did not become an immediate hit.

experiences rejection – financial and societal – and only ultimately finds peace in death. There's an easy informality and rich texture to the duo's harmonies here, and it's all underpinned and propelled along by strident double bass: "Who will love a little Sparrow? / Who's traveled far and cries for rest? / 'Not I', said the Oak Tree / 'I won't share my branches with no sparrow's nest / And my blanket of leaves won't warm her cold breast.'"

Benedictus
Cello and a sparse guitar serve as the accompaniment on this final track on side one, a composition adapted from a two-part acapella motet by 16th century Flemish composer, Orlande de Lassus. It's a beautiful work, more redolent of a psalm, with Art and Paul's seamless harmonies shifting and ascending effortlessly, enhanced by the rich, deep timbre of the cello that underpins them.

The Sound of Silence
The song that launched Simon and Garfunkel and without which, they could arguably have been little more than a footnote in musical history. When *Wednesday Morning, 3 A.M.* was released on 19 October, 1964, it was a commercial failure prompting Simon to return to England and Garfunkel to resume his studies at Columbia University. But

> **Simon and Garfunkel were now firmly entranced by the folk revival**

Credit: Alamy, Getty Images, Adobe Stock

Discography

by 1965 this track began picking up airplay in Boston and on radio stations throughout Florida. The growing interest prompted Tom Wilson to remix the track, adding electric guitars, bass and drums. In the week ending 1 January 1966, the remixed version hit No.1 in the *Billboard* Hot 100 chart, prompting the duo to hastily reform. From the haunting reverb-soaked opening line "Hello darkness my old friend", this is an anthem for troubled times, a soaring emotive beacon of hope and one of the greatest folk songs ever written. The remix is the one we all remember but this original, acoustic version is arguably as potent and memorable.

He Was My Brother

This was one of Simon's oldest compositions and the one that convinced Tom Wilson to sign the duo. It focuses on the death of a Freedom Rider and was dedicated to Andrew Jacobs, Simon's Queens College classmate and civil rights activist who was murdered by the Ku Klux Klan along with two other people. The jaunty acoustic strumming belies the poignancy of the song and its deeply personal lyrics: "Freedom Rider / They cursed my brother to his face / Go home outsider / This town's gonna be your buryin' place". It's a potent track, with its direct, literal lyrics infused with an angry yet life-affirming message.

Peggy-O

A likeable adaptation of the Scottish folk song 'The Bonnie Lass O' Fyvie' about a thwarted romance between a soldier and a girl. Simon & Garfunkel imbue a real purity into the song, their hushed harmonies giving the track a lush intimacy, every phrase and syllable sensitively enunciated for real emotive effect: "As we marched down to Fennario / As we marched down to Fennario / Our captain fell in love / With a lady like a dove / And they called her name pretty Peggy-O." Bob Dylan and Joan Baez had already recorded versions of this song, in 1962 and 1963 respectively.

Go Tell It on the Mountain

There's a real breezy 60s pop feel to this otherwise uninspiring spiritual. Once again, The Everly Brothers' vocal harmony sound dominates, but there is little to really elevate what is essentially a deeply traditional religious composition. The duo and their producer Tom Wilson bring nothing creative or new to the song and so it sounds benign, simply a retelling of what had gone before. By the time of this album's release in October

The pair performing at The Bitter End in Greenwich Village the day after the album was released.

Wednesday Morning, 3 A.M.

1964, The Beatles were storming the US charts and rendering tracks such as this woefully outdated in the context of the young generation.

The Sun Is Burning

There are dark lyrical undercurrents within this composition by respected British folk musician Ian Campbell: "Now the sun has come to earth / Shrouded in a mushroom cloud of death / Death comes in a blinding flash / Of hellish heat and leaves a smear of ash / And the sun has come to earth". Essentially, the song is a metaphor for nuclear war. Campbell had wanted the British folk movement to take a stand against nuclear war and all his early proceeds from his version went to the Campaign for Nuclear Disarmament. Like Campbell's version, Simon & Garfunkel's is soft and intimate, which only highlights the potency of the lyrical content.

The Times They Are A-Changin'

Bob Dylan's influence was all pervasive on the folk scene by this point and so it's no surprise that the duo cover the title track from his 1964 album of the same name. By the time they recorded *Wednesday Morning, 3 A.M.*, Simon's own writing style had developed beyond Dylan's influence as he began to define his own sound. This is a faithful and far less fiery rendition of this landmark Dylan song, delivered with a straighter traditional folk approach. Interestingly, it's Garfunkel's harmony that dominates in the mix at times, resulting in Simon's top line melody being somewhat obscured. It's an affectionate cover and has real charms.

Wednesday Morning, 3 A.M.

On this title track, the narrator lies in bed next to his sleeping partner, reflecting on a crime he has committed: "For I know with the first light of dawn / I'll be leaving / And tonight will be / All I have left to recall". Simon's intricate picking and the double bass are engaging but it's inevitably the beautifully restrained and tender harmonies that hold the listener's attention. As a song, it's arguably not fully formed, but it points the way to the defiantly unique sound that the two young men from the borough of Queens were forging. The album was a commercial flop, prompting the duo to split up. But their prodigious talent and Tom Wilson's tenacity would ensure that they would reform for a second album, with Simon continuing to lay the foundations for a stellar catalogue of songs that would launch them onto the international stage.

Simon & Garfunkel are among the many artists to have covered Bob Dylan's 'The Times They Are a-Changin''.

> **They were forging a defiantly unique sound**

Credit: Alamy, Getty Images, Adobe Stock

Struggles, perseverance and a couple of doomed early albums: the world just wasn't ready for Simon & Garfunkel in 1964 and '65…

One & Done?

WORDS BY **ROGER DAVIES**

On paper, the future looked bright for Paul Simon and Art Garfunkel as 1963 became 1964. Columbia's Tom Wilson had arranged a contract for the duo, who now stepped away from their former sequence of stage names and performed as Simon & Garfunkel for the first time; they went down well at a promotional showcase in New York on 31 March '64; and their first album, *Wednesday Morning, 3 A.M.*, was recorded the same month. Surely the world was there for the taking for these diffident, 22-year-old law and mathematics students?

Well, perhaps not just yet. Even though the subtitle of *Wednesday Morning, 3 A.M.* promised 'Exciting new sounds in the folk tradition', the American public didn't buy it, literally or metaphorically. The album, made up of five Simon songs and seven more or less gentle folk songs from the acoustic tradition, was a commercial failure, selling only 3,000 copies on its release in October 1964. One of its songs, the original acoustic version of 'The Sound of Silence' – titled 'The Sounds of Silence' in this incarnation – was released as a single, but also failed to make an impact.

Why was this? Well, consider the music that was coming out in late '64. The world was now two years into Beatlemania, especially in the US, where the Liverpool quartet were spearheading the British Invasion. The Beatles were in their *Hard Day's Night* pomp, delivering amped-up rock'n'roll and vivid ballads, a world away from the delicate acoustic lisping of *Wednesday Morning, 3 A.M.* The Rolling Stones were stealing headlines as they toured America; Bob Dylan was taking the intellectual folk world by storm; and big, brassy soul bands such as The Supremes were all over the airwaves. Who could hope to compete against such huge talents?

Faced with their album's underperformance, the duo effectively split up, with both men returning to academia. Garfunkel went back to Columbia University to complete his degree in mathematics, while Simon resumed his studies at Brooklyn Law

In 1964, Garfunkel returned to Columbia University, while Simon briefly returned to law school.

School, at least partly because his parents wanted him to do so. He only completed the autumn 1964 semester, though, defying his elders and betters by returning to England in January '65, determined to make a go of a career in music this time. This was, you will agree, a wise decision.

A factor in Simon's return to the UK was that he had enjoyed some mild success over here as a songwriter. A song that he had written in 1963 under the name Paul Kane, 'Carlos Dominguez', had

25

Chapter 1

1960s folk-rock artists struggled to compete with rock'n'roll groups of the British Invasion.

The Paul Simon Songbook cover featured Simon's then girlfriend, Kathy Chitty.

been licensed by a publishing company called Lorna Music and covered by the pop crooner Val Doonican, who had done well out of it. Simon visited the Lorna Music offices to express his gratitude over the release, and was offered a publishing and recording contract. A deal followed with the Oriole label, for which he recorded a single of his own called 'He's My Brother'.

Simon used his time wisely while in London, it must be said. Playing folk clubs and doing a lot of what we would refer to today as networking, he soon became friends with established British folkies such as Bert Jansch, Martin Carthy, Al 'Year of the Cat' Stewart and Sandy Denny, later of the Strawbs and Fairport Convention. He also gained notice as early as 27 January 1965 when the BBC featured him on its *Five to Ten* morning radio show, playing a set of 13 songs and discussing their origins. The unlikely back-story here is that the BBC first heard of Simon when his landlady, a helpful social worker called Judith Piepe, sent in a tape of the songs he'd done for the Lorna company.

An album deal followed with CBS, which had absorbed Simon's label Oriole, and the scene was set for a Paul Simon solo album: the previous year's underwhelming *Wednesday Morning, 3 A.M.* was regarded as an irrelevance as the LP had not been released in Britain. He recorded his new songs in June 1965 in London with Tom Wilson at the helm, titling his LP *The Paul Simon Songbook* and including songs that fans will recognise such as 'I Am a Rock' and 'April Come She Will'.

The new album, released in August, didn't exactly set the charts alight, but it certainly helped Simon build a profile, along with live dates that he performed in England, France, Holland and Denmark that summer. A single release of 'I Am a Rock' kept momentum gently rolling, and Simon decided to remain in London to continue his career.

It was at this point that an unlikely guardian angel in the form of Tom Wilson intervened. Through the summer of 1965, Wilson had noticed that the original, acoustic 'The Sounds of Silence' was starting to enjoy radio airplay in certain American markets, namely Boston and Florida, inspiring him to re-record the song as a new version. Retaining the original's ethereal vocals, he added electric guitars, bass and drums to create a strident, utterly persuasive anthem that presented Simon & Garfunkel in a whole new light – one much more attuned to the rock audience of the day.

The new song, renamed 'The Sound of Silence', was released on 12 September 1965. Could such a ruse even hope to work? Let's see…

Simon posing for a photo during his time in London, May 1965.

" *Simon used his time wisely while in London*

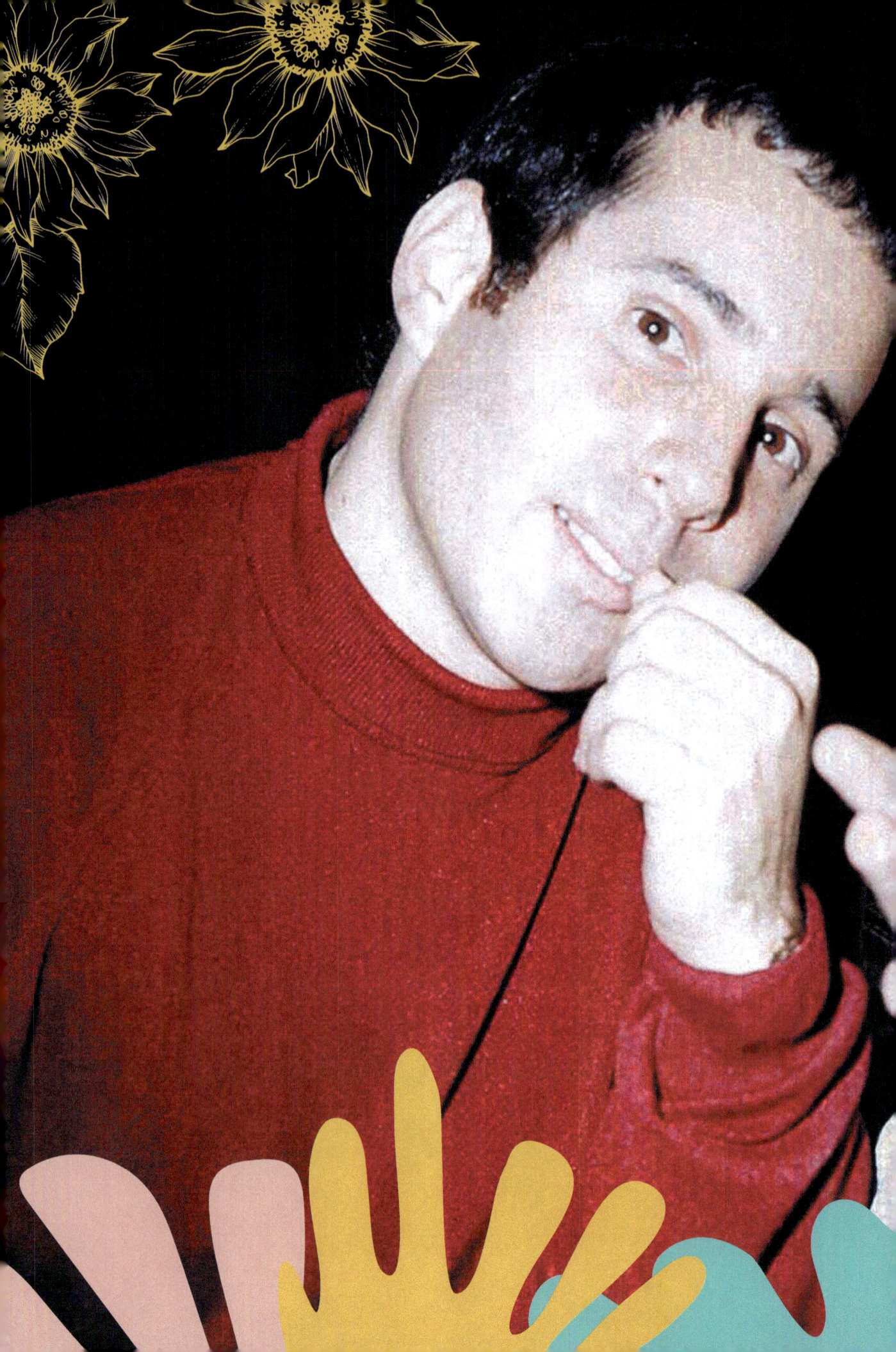

Chapter 2

- **30** THE SOUND OF SUCCESS
- **38** SOUNDS OF SILENCE (1966)
- **42** PARSLEY, SAGE, ROSEMARY AND THYME (1966)
- **46** THE GRADUATE SOUNDTRACK
- **50** BOOKENDS (1968)
- **54** THE BEGINNING OF THE END
- **60** BRIDGE OVER TROUBLED WATER (1970)

Credit: Shutterstock

On top of the world in 1966, Simon & Garfunkel reigned as rulers of folk-rock. Few other artists have ever matched the output of this imperial phase

WORDS BY **JOEL McIVER**

The Sound of Success

Folk-rock, as a musical genre, was the creation of a few gifted musicians and producers, the former of whom wrote great songs and the latter of whom saw a way to make those songs widely desirable to the public. The folk-rock family tree was planted by Bob Dylan, grew via Simon & Garfunkel, bore fruit with James Taylor and then spread overseas with British groups such as Fairport Convention.

To extend the arboreal metaphor, its head gardener was producer Tom Wilson, who took the early sound of Bob Dylan, beefed it up with electric instruments for a rock'n'roll touch, and in doing so sold it to Sixties music lovers in huge quantities, before repeating this trick with 'The Sound of Silence'.

Rolling Stone defined Wilson's role perfectly when they wrote of Dylan's new sound: "By fusing the Chuck Berry beat of The Rolling Stones and The Beatles with the leftist, folk tradition of the folk revival, Dylan really had brought it back home, creating a new kind of rock and roll… that made every type of artistic tradition available to rock."

Curiously, Wilson's own reflection on the new genre makes it clear that folk wasn't exactly dear to his heart, at least at first: as he said, "I didn't even particularly like folk music. I'd been recording Sun Ra and John Coltrane… I thought folk music was for the dumb guys. Dylan played like the dumb guys, but then these words came out. I was flabbergasted."

Of course, this neat evolution wasn't apparent to Paul Simon and Art Garfunkel when, in January 1966, they learned that the new, Wilson-re-recorded version of 'The Sound of Silence' was at Number One in the American charts. Neither Wilson nor the Columbia label had bothered to tell them that the new version existed, let alone that it had been released, and Simon in particular is

Chapter 2

said to have been taken aback – or even horrified, depending on which source you believe – when he first heard it.

Art Garfunkel wasn't keen either. "It was in that electric 12-string style of The Byrds," he told *Blue Railroad* magazine. "It's cute. They've drowned out the strength of the lyric and they've made it more of a fashion kind of production. And you never know. I was mildly amused and detached with the certainty that it was not a hit. I don't have hits."

His view of the song mellowed over the years, however, as well it might. "Ah, what a tune!" Garfunkel told MusicRadar in 2012. "'Sound of Silence' has more melodic, genius, simple power than I ever realised. As the years go by, there's something extraordinarily hooky about that simple melody – I didn't know that. I knew it was a good-sounding record when it emerged… It was the sixth song Paul ever wrote. He would come to my apartment on Amsterdam Avenue, where the roaches were in the kitchen, and he'd play me his songs. When he got to this one, I said, 'Best one yet!'"

Many tracks on *Sounds of Silence* were written by Simon during his time in London.

What did the man who actually wrote the song think of it? Well, it seems that Paul Simon has a mixed relationship with 'The Sound of Silence'. It launched his career, as we'll see, but it must have been galling that it was only in re-recorded form – and without his direct involvement – that the song became popular. It's hard to imagine any creative person being fully reconciled to such a manoeuvre, even though it brought huge fame and fortune.

You can read about Simon's complex view of the song between the lines of

To capitalise on Simon & Garfunkel's growing popularity, *Wednesday Morning, 3 A.M.* was re-released in January '66.

'The Sound of Silence' was pivotal in Simon & Garfunkel's success – it was the track that got them signed to Columbia, and later made them famous.

> " **It was only in its re-recorded form that 'The Sound of Silence' became popular**

Chapter 2

Simon & Garfunkel in concert at Toronto's Massey Hall, January 1967.

an interview with *NPR*, in which he explained: "The key to 'The Sound of Silence' is the simplicity of the melody and the words, which are youthful alienation. It's a young lyric, but not bad for a 21-year-old. It's not a sophisticated thought, but a thought that I gathered from some college reading material or something. It wasn't something that I was experiencing at some deep, profound level – nobody's listening to me, nobody's listening to anyone – it was a post-adolescent angst, but it had some level of truth to it and it resonated with millions of people, largely because it had a simple and singable melody."

The primary consequence of the sudden, unexpected hit song – which swiftly sold over a million copies – was, of course, that Simon & Garfunkel had to react quickly or their newfound momentum would be lost. To this end, they regrouped in New York to discuss their next move: Garfunkel later recalled that Simon left the UK with understandable reluctance.

"He was in love with Kathy [Chitty, his girlfriend] and England, and his life as a free young Yankee," Garfunkel said. "And he hated to have to relate to a hit record in America. Even though it was the thing we had long wanted, it came at an unfortunate time. It was the winter of '65. And he only knew that it was happening when it broke the Top 10. So Paul came home, we met in the basement, we said, 'All right, this thing we've been looking for all these years has finally happened. It behoves us to be smart and see if we could have a follow-up hit'."

Columbia immediately insisted that the duo follow up 'The Sound of Silence' with a full album, hoping for a major hit this time rather than a repeat of the dud *Wednesday Morning, 3 A.M.* Just in case, the company reissued the *3 A.M.* album in January 1966, but once again, it didn't make much of an impression.

The two songwriters were happy to oblige, but they didn't want their next single to be a simple 'Sound of Silence' clone. As Garfunkel explained, "We turned all our attention to what would be the single we would put out, to secure this toe-hold we had in the business. To show people it wasn't a fluke and to show people we could make an interesting record in a whole other vein. So our goal was to have a hit that was nothing like 'The Sound of Silence'… just to show chart muscle in a different way."

You can read more about the resulting album, named *Sounds of Silence* at the record company's insistence, elsewhere in this publication. Let's just say here that in recording and releasing an LP as well-crafted as this one in record time, Simon & Garfunkel pulled off a miracle. Released on 17 January 1966, the LP mostly consisted of reworked songs from Simon's solo album *The Paul Simon Songbook*, plus a few new cuts, and made Number 21 on the *Billboard* chart – a moderate rather than massive success, but one significant enough to keep the duo rolling forward.

Live dates now opened up for the rest of the year and beyond, with

The Sound of Success

professional management and booking agents secured for Simon & Garfunkel. The reception to the newly hot duo was mostly positive, although one or two critics carped about the twosome not being 'folk' enough – or simply being too influenced by Bob Dylan's sound to be taken seriously. Simon had always paid due credit to Dylan, in his defence, but he had little need to do so: vocally, the two golden-voiced singers were on another planet to the former Robert Zimmerman, and their politics were also much less confrontational than his.

In a sense, Paul Simon's lyrics encompassed more universal themes than those of Dylan, too. On 17 February, the duo played a Canadian TV broadcast called *Let's Sing Out*, a specialist folk programme filmed at the University of Toronto that connected college audiences with new musicians. On air, Simon explained of 'The Sound of Silence': "One of the biggest hangups we have today is the inability of people to communicate, not only on an intellectual level, but on an emotional level as well. So you have people unable to touch other people, unable to love other people. And this is a song about the inability to communicate." It's interesting that his words are doubly relevant today, when personal contact has at least partly been replaced by communications technology.

In May, two more singles were released: the triumphant 'Homeward Bound' and the anthemic 'I Am a Rock', both of which broke into the American Top Ten. These were the new types of 'chart muscle' that Garfunkel referred to above: completely different in energy level and mood than the reflective 'The Sound of Silence', they showed the world another side of Simon & Garfunkel that was critically and commercially acclaimed.

In the late Sixties, artists were expected to issue more than one album a year if they wanted to retain their fans' attention – and so it was that pressure came to bear on Simon & Garfunkel to come up with a follow-up to *Sounds of Silence*, the quicker the better. Knowing full well that *Sounds...* had been rushed out to a cynically tight deadline, the two men insisted on taking their time

The duo embarked on a US tour to support *Sounds of Silence*.

A performance on the British music show *Ready Steady Go!* in July 1965.

Simon & Garfunkel's manager, Mort Lewis, would only allow television appearances on the condition that they were allowed to choose the setlist or play an uninterrupted set.

The Sound of Success

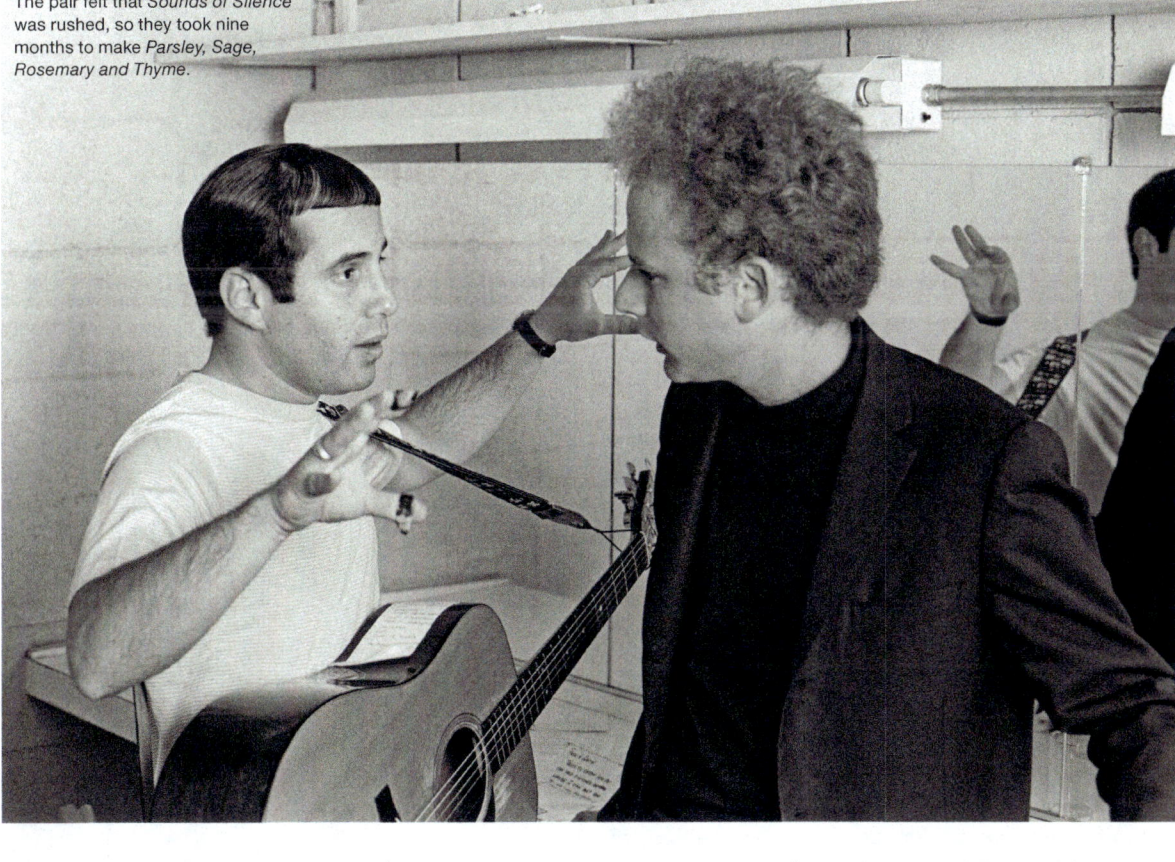

The pair felt that *Sounds of Silence* was rushed, so they took nine months to make *Parsley, Sage, Rosemary and Thyme*.

over album number three, *Parsley, Sage, Rosemary and Thyme*, which was released in October 1966.

They were right to do so. As you can read elsewhere, *Parsley...* is a finely crafted album packed with career-defining songs, from the earlier single 'Homeward Bound' to 'The 59th Street Bridge Song (Feelin' Groovy)' and beyond. By now Simon & Garfunkel were performing regularly on TV, although these appearances were tightly controlled by their manager Mort Lewis, who insisted that the duo retain artistic control at all times.

It seemed at this point in the young singers' lives that everything was going to plan, but the first obstacle to the duo's progress struck in early 1967 when Simon developed writer's block. Columbia executives and Garfunkel, who was never a songwriter, stood patiently – and then impatiently – by, while Simon wrestled with his condition. At one point, Columbia's chairman Clive Davis gave the twosome an encouraging pep-talk, hoping to inspire some productivity; they are said to have recorded the conversation in order to mock it later.

The year 1967 was one of the greatest, if not the greatest, in popular music history, with the Summer of Love, The Beatles' momentous *Sgt. Pepper's Lonely Hearts Club Band* album and the apex of psychedelic hippiedom all in alignment – and yet Simon & Garfunkel appeared to be attending the party on a strictly part-time basis. Could nothing be done to resolve the situation?

Fortunately, Hollywood stepped in to save the day.

On stage at the Monterey Pop Festival in California, June 1967.

Credit: Alamy, Getty Images

Discography

SOUNDS OF SILENCE

Released 17 January 1966
Words by Neil Crossley

On their second album, Simon & Garfunkel embrace the emerging folk-rock style and unveil an album with a clutch of timeless classics

The Sound of Silence
Eighteen months after unveiling their debut long player, the duo released their second album, a work that is light years ahead of the unassuming acoustic compositions of its predecessor. By then a landmark new genre dubbed 'folk-rock' had emerged, spearheaded by bands such as The Byrds and Buffalo Springfield. This electric version of 'The Sound of Silence', which had already scored a No.1 hit, fitted seamlessly into the amplified, more driven sound of the day. With this gem already in place, the duo, along with producers Tom Wilson and Bob Johnston, set about creating an album that would fly on the coat-tails of the new folk-rock sound.

Leaves That Are Green
This melodic ballad was originally written and recorded by Paul Simon for his 1965 album *The Paul Simon Songbook* but was re-recorded with Art Garfunkel for inclusion on this album, adding electric harpsichord, rhythm guitar and bass. There's a sprightly, folk-pop feel to the track, with its gently skittering percussion. Lyrically it focuses on the ever-constant aging process, using nature as a reference for life and death. The song became the B-side for the 'Homeward Bound' single. Seventeen years later, the opening lines, "I was 21 years when I wrote this song / I'm 22 now but I won't be for long," would be used by Billy Bragg for his single 'New England'.

Blessed
This track features strong echoes of The Byrds' single 'Turn, Turn, Turn', which was an international hit by the time this was recorded on 21 December 1965. Both tracks have strong religious themes and 'Blessed' features a similar descending chord sequence – in this case G-F#m-Em-D – on the line "For they shall inherit". It sounds like a song that has been sonically contrived for the era, with its discordant electric guitar and sitar-like drones. It has its merits but has not stood the test of time and is arguably one of the weakest tracks on the album.

Kathy's Song
Another song that originally appeared on Simon's 1965 solo album and was re-recorded for *Sounds of Silence*. This song is dedicated to Kathy Chitty, his girlfriend and muse during his mid-60s sojourn to England. It's a classic Simon & Garfunkel recording, one of Simon's most personal compositions, and has appeared on most of their compilation albums. It's beautiful, heartfelt and honest, and widely regarded as one of Simon's most personal songs. Gentle picked Spanish guitar is the sole accompaniment and the lyrics are peppered with references to the person and country he has left behind: "And from the shelter of my mind / Through the window of my eyes / I gaze beyond the rain-drenched streets / To England where my heart lies".

Somewhere They Can't Find Me
Essentially this is a reworking of the title track of *Wednesday Morning, 3 A.M.* and it's a far more strident and successful affair. The narrator lies in bed next to his sleeping partner, deeply regretful of

Sounds of Silence

a crime he has committed. But whereas in the original version the tone was introspective, here it is assertive, set against electric instrumentation and a 4/4 shuffle beat. Paul and Artie's vocals are strong and tightly delivered as they detail the loss and regret that permeate the lyrical narrative: "Oh, my life seems unreal, my crime an illusion / A scene badly written in which I must play / And thought it puts me up tight to leave you / I know it's not right to leave you / When morning is just a few hours away."

> **"A landmark new genre dubbed 'folk-rock' had emerged**

Anji
A rare instrumental outing for Simon & Garfunkel and a cover of an acoustic fingerstyle guitar piece, written and recorded in 1961 by British guitarist and folk revival stalwart, Davey Graham. A number of notable artists such as Bert Jansch would also cover the track and his version appeared in 1965 on his eponymous debut album. There's a pacey ragtime feel to the track, with its infectious, descending bassline. This composition serves as a reminder of just

The success of 'The Sound of Silence' brought Simon & Garfunkel back to the studio.

Simon and Garfunkel made their first and only appearance on *The Ed Sullivan Show* on 30 January 1966.

Sounds of Silence

The pair pictured at the Columbia Records offices in New York.

how assured and nimble a guitarist Paul Simon actually is.

Richard Cory
The song was based on Edwin Arlington Robinson's 1897 poem of the same name, recounting the story of the character of industrialist Richard Cory from the perspective of a man who works in his factory. Deep envy of Cory's wealth and advantages pervades the lyrics: "The papers print his pictures almost everywhere he goes / Richard Cory at the opera, Richard Cory at a show / And the rumour of his parties and the orgies on his yacht / Oh, he surely must be happy with everything he's got." Backing is provided by Joe South, while legendary session player Hal Blaine is behind the drum kit.

A Most Peculiar Man
Loneliness and isolation are prevailing lyrical themes on 'A Most Peculiar Man', which features lush guitar jangle and sitar-style flourishes. The wry observational lyrics and social realism evoke The Kinks and The Beatles, particularly *Rubber Soul*, which was released in December 1965. Almost six decades on, it retains a real period charm, bolstered by Simon's vocals, which have a real sardonic edge: "He was a most peculiar man / That's what Mrs Reardon says, and she should know / She lived upstairs from him / She said he was a most peculiar man".

April Come She Will
Along with 'Kathy's Song', this is one of the most personal tracks on the album. Simon wrote the song while in England in 1964 and it was inspired by a girl he met and the nursery rhyme she used to recite. Simon used the changing seasons as a metaphor for the girl's changing moods. The song is included on the soundtrack for *The Graduate* and is used in the pool scene in the film. It was also the B-side for the hit single 'Scarborough Fair / Canticle'. It's the shortest song on the album but one of the finest, with a purity and sense of yearning underpinned by its lean melodic structure: "April, come she will / When streams are ripe and swelled with rain / May, she will stay / Resting in my arms again."

We've Got a Groovy Thing Goin'
Recorded on 5 April 1965 on the same session as 'Somewhere They Can't Find Me', this is a full-on production piece and one of the rockier tracks on the album, with brass stabs, stop-starts and heaps of echo. Simon had returned from his extended stay in England with a bulging notebook of new material and this was one of them. At its heart it's an unashamed novelty pop song and sounds like it could have come out of the Brill Building. It's propelled by a driving 4/4 beat and is mildly reminiscent of Ray Charles 'What'd I Say?', but without the groove. Compared to the track that precedes it, this is lightweight but it's strident and joyous: "You must be out of your mind / Do you know what you're kickin' away? / We've got a groovy thing goin', baby."

I Am a Rock
Isolation and emotional detachment are the underlying themes of the concluding track on the album, which was released as a single in 1966 and featured as the B-side of the 1971 A-side reissue of 'The 59th Street Bridge Song'. The upbeat nature of the song belies its insular underbelly as Simon recounts the tale of a man who refuses to socialise with others. As ever, there is a beautiful timbre and resonance to Simon's vocal, which melds flawlessly with Garfunkel's stellar harmony work: "I have my books / And my poetry to protect me / I am shielded in my armour / Hiding in my room safe within my womb / I touch no one and no one touches me / I am a rock, I am an island."

Credit: Alamy, Getty Images, Adobe Stock

Discography

PARSLEY, SAGE, ROSEMARY AND THYME

Released 24 October 1966
Words by Neil Crossley

A beguiling era-defining release that is widely, and rightly, regarded as the duo's first masterpiece

The album was unusually expensive to make, due to the pair's extended studio time.

Scarborough Fair / Canticle

In a move wholly at odds with the ethos of most folk musicians, Simon & Garfunkel spent over three months in the studio honing this third album. The duo insisted on full creative control, focusing on production and instrumentation and working alongside engineer Roy Halee. They persuaded Columbia Records to provide an eight-track recorder and all vocal takes were overdubbed to increase the separation between Simon's vocal and guitar. The album opens with one of the last vestiges of Simon's time in England, adapted from an arrangement that he had learned from folk stalwart Martin Carthy. *Scarborough Fair* can be traced back as far as 1670, while *Canticle* was reworking of an earlier Simon composition. Combined, they make for a beautifully ornate composition, whose status would be cemented by its inclusion in the 1967 film *The Graduate*.

Patterns

This is one of three songs that first appeared on Simon's 1965 album *The Paul Simon Songbook*. Lyrically, it focuses on how life can be a labyrinthine maze, creating patterns that can be difficult to unravel or control. There's a real sense of wonder to his vocal delivery and a raw, unbridled feel to his playing, which is underpinned by echo-soaked congas, and fluid, percussive bass. As is the case across this album, there are some tasteful, inspired production touches. In many ways, this album is a sonic achievement that is up there with The Beatles' *Revolver* and The Beach Boys' *Pet Sounds*.

Cloudy

Spanish-influenced flourishes of guitar intro this track, which was co-written by Paul Simon and Bruce Woodley of The Seekers. Like many compositions on the album, its twists and turns are rarely predictable. Just when you sense that the track is opening up into a grand production, it pulls back. The arrangement is lean, with every element being made to count. Lyrically, it is widescreen and evocative: "My thoughts are scattered and they're cloudy / They have no borders, no boundaries / They echo and they swell / From Tolstoy to Tinker Bell / Down from Berkeley to Carmel / Got some pictures in my pocket and a lot of time to kill".

Homeward Bound

Legend has it that Simon wrote this song on a railway station in Widnes, following a gig in Liverpool in 1965, although some doubt has been cast on this. In 2001, Geoff Speed, who provided lodgings for Simon in Liverpool, told *The Guardian*: "It is probable he wrote one verse in Liverpool and the chorus in Wigan, with the song being finished in Widnes." We heard him writing the tune when he was staying at our house and then we dropped him at the station. He probably finished the song on the platform." Few songs have captured the melancholy and homesickness of a travelling musician like this one: "Every day's an endless stream / Of cigarettes and magazines / And each town looks the same to me / The movies and the factories / And every stranger's face I see / Reminds me that I long to be / Homeward bound". The song became a No.5 hit in the *Billboard Hot 100* and reached No.9 in the UK.

Parsley, Sage, Rosemary and Thyme

Performing 'Scarborough Fair' with Andy Williams on his *Kaleidoscope Company* musical special, April 1968.

The Big Bright Green Pleasure Machine

Another song penned during Simon's time in England in 1965 and allegedly written while he sat in a laundrette watching his clothes spin round. The song takes a cynical swipe at Madison Avenue, epicentre of the US advertising industry. It also references the hippie movement and the Vietnam War, as well as honing in on various unanswered personal questions. This track reflects the fact that songs were darker and deeper than before. In a retrospective review for AllMusic, Matthew Greenwald describes the track as "a great putdown song about the effect of television".

The 59th Street Bridge Song (Feelin' Groovy)

A sparkling skip of a track that reportedly came to Paul Simon during a walk across New York's Queensboro Bridge, which joins Manhattan and Queens. The line "Just kicking down the cobblestones" references the paving at the approach to the bridge's Queens end. It has an infectious descending chord sequence and four bars in, Dave Brubeck Quartet members Joe Morello (drums) and Eugene Wright (bass) kick in. Despite the memorable, toe-tapping feel, the running time of just 1 minute 47 seconds was deemed too short for radio airplay. None of which concerned Paul Simon. "Sometimes I make a song purely an impression," he told the *New Yorker* in September, 1967. "When you've made your impression, stop."

The Dangling Conversation

Released in September 1966 as the second single from the album, this song did not perform as well as the duo hoped, peaking at No.25 in the US. Simon was profoundly disappointed and told *Record Mirror* that it was "above the kids" and perhaps "too heavy for a mainstream audience". Intricate motifs on Spanish guitar intro the track, before bass and cello enter the mix. Lyrically, it's easy to see how the references to revered poets Emily

As with their previous album, *Parsley*... also included songs originally recorded for *The Paul Simon Songbook*.

" **Simon apes Dylan's vocal nuances perfectly**

Parsley, Sage, Rosemary and Thyme

Dickinson and Robert Frost might be too obscure for a mainstream audience. But it remains a beautiful, heartfelt track.

Flowers Never Bend with the Rainfall

This song finds Paul Simon at his most philosophical and reflective, musing on age and the passing of time. It's a pacey, strident track, with an ascending G-Bm-C chord structure on the verses and bluegrass and country tinges throughout: "Through the corridors of sleep / Past shadows dark and deep / My mind dances and leaps in confusion / I don't know what is real / I can't touch what I feel / And I hide behind the shield of my illusion." It's a decidedly more spartan production from the duo, which suits the purity of the track.

A Simple Desultory Philippic

Generally believed to be a parody of Bob Dylan, this was another track that appeared on the 1965 album *The Paul Simon Songbook*. The original version was subtitled *(Or how I was Lyndon Johnson'd into Submission)*. Sprightly descending bass and Hammond B3 organ stabs underpin this track and Simon apes Dylan's vocal nuances perfectly on a song that references cultural luminaries of the day: "I been Norman Mailered, Maxwell Taylored / I been John O'Hara'd, McNamara'd / I been Rolling Stoned and Beatled 'til I'm blind / I been Ayn Randed, nearly branded / Communist, 'cause I'm left-handed / That's the hand I use, well, never mind". A wry and charming song.

For Emily, Whenever I May Find Her

Deep, rich vocal reverb and a 12-string acoustic guitar are features of this track, which is sung solely by Art Garfunkel. Theories abound on who is the inspiration for the song. Poet Emily Dickinson has been suggested although Simon's relationship with Kathy Chitty seems another likely source. It's an ethereal, mystical-sounding song and a showpiece for Garfunkel's intense and beautifully tender vocal performance. Running at just 2:05 it's a real masterclass in the less-is-more approach to production and arrangement. Lyrically, it is haunting and evocative: "And when you ran to me / Your cheeks flushed with the night / We walked on frosted fields / of juniper and lamplight / I held your hand".

A Poem on the Underground Wall

A graffiti artist on the London Underground is the inspiration for this song, another penned during Simon's time in England in 1965. A single kick drum intros the track, evoking the rhythmic motion of train wheels on a track. This segues into intricate and pacey Spanish guitar patterns over which the duo's rich, textural harmonies float. It's a simple narrative, almost childlike at times, but it all makes for an engaging whole: "The last train is nearly due / The underground is closing soon / And in the dark deserted station / Restless in anticipation / A man waits in the shadows."

7 O'Clock News / Silent Night

A gentle piano arpeggio provides the accompaniment for Simon & Garfunkel's hushed rendition of the classic Yuletide carol, over which runs a recording of a TV anchorman reading the news. It's an intriguingly subversive juxtaposition, one that lends weight and credence to the album by acknowledging the tumultuous times in which it was recorded. Martin Luther King Jr, the Civil Rights Bill, Nixon's push for the Vietnam War and the death of Lenny Bruce are all namechecked. The simple purity of their voices set against such chilling era-defining moments provide an edgy, yet crowning conclusion to this majestic and timeless album.

The duo promoted their album on the college circuit in the US.

Credit: Alamy, Getty Images, Adobe Stock

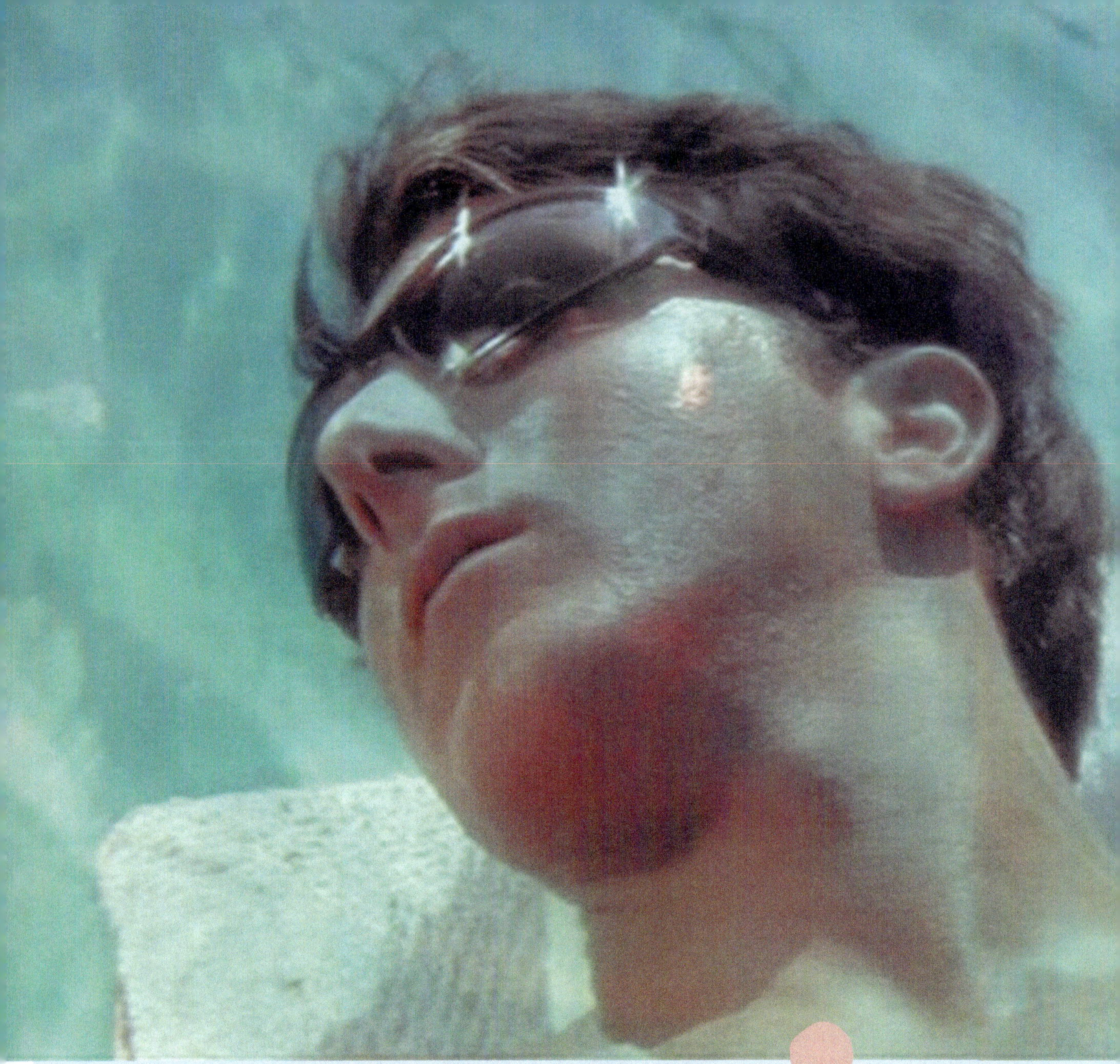

The Graduate soundtrack

So here's to you, Mr Nichols… Simon & Garfunkel's fans love you more than you will know. Whoa-ho-ho!

WORDS BY **JOEL McIVER**

Paul Simon and Dustin Hoffman looked unnervingly alike in their younger years: handsome in a collegiate way, vertically challenged, and dark haired with a generous coiffure. This makes it all the more unusual that an identical commercial hit in both men's early careers came in the form of the 1967 movie *The Graduate*. In fact, the film and the best-known song which Simon & Garfunkel contributed to its soundtrack – 'Mrs Robinson', as you surely know if you're reading this – are inseparable.

Still, this serendipitous partnership might never have occurred. As we've seen, Paul Simon was suffering from writer's block in 1967, but that didn't mean he was ready to jump right onto any project that was offered to him. The director, Mike Nichols, was a huge Simon & Garfunkel fan and had persuaded Columbia big cheese Clive Davis on board with the *Graduate* project, but Simon needed a little more convincing. Nichols was a stage veteran, for sure, and had made a decent debut film in *Who's Afraid of Virginia Woolf?* (1966) but he wasn't the star director he later became, simply because he hadn't made *The Graduate* yet.

Fortunately, Simon eventually signed up, not uncoincidentally relieved from his writer's block by a cheque for $25,000

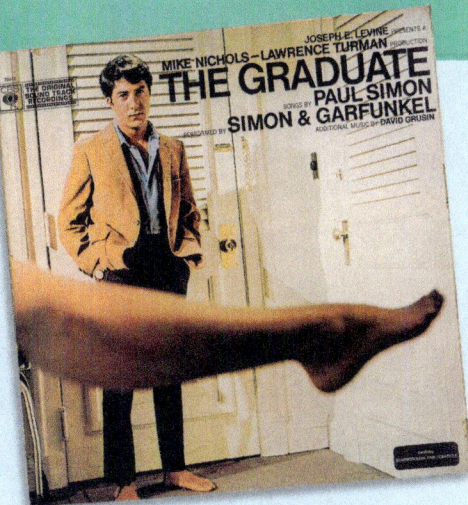

The Graduate soundtrack introduced Simon & Garfunkel's music to a wider audience beyond folk-rock fans.

Chapter 2

(worth a sweet quarter of a million bucks today) for three songs. The first two he sent over to Nichols were 'Punky's Dilemma' and 'Overs', which failed to impress the director – but the third, 'Mrs Robinson', quite rightly had him foaming at the mouth with enthusiasm.

The song originated as a work-in-progress that Simon had tentatively called 'Mrs Roosevelt', and played in its unfinished form to Nichols, who loved it. The director later recalled, "They filled in with dee de dee dee de dee dee dee because there was no verse yet, but I liked even that."

Art Garfunkel elaborated: "Paul had been working on what is now 'Mrs Robinson', but there was no name in it and we'd just fill in with any three-syllable name. And because of the character in the picture, we just began using the name 'Mrs Robinson' to fit... and one day we were sitting around with Mike, talking about ideas for another song. And I said 'What about 'Mrs Robinson'?' Mike shot to his feet. 'You have a song called 'Mrs Robinson' and you haven't even shown it to me?' So we explained the working title and sang it for him. And then Mike froze it for the picture as 'Mrs Robinson'."

It's a perfect song for the movie, which is the story of a weird, doomed love tryst between a recently graduated 21-year-old called Benjamin Braddock (Hoffman), his girlfriend Elaine (Katharine Ross) and his girlfriend's mother Mrs Robinson (Anne Bancroft). The last of these is a classic silver-screen anti-heroine: a beautiful, predatory diva who pretty much ruins Braddock's life, even though he and Elaine run away together at the end. Audiences and critics loved the film, rewarding Nichols' efforts with the highest box-office grosses of 1967 and seven Oscar nominations, of which he won Best Director. Nichols went on to be one of only 18 EGOT winners – top-flight creatives who have been awarded an Emmy, Grammy, Oscar and Tony award – and died in 2014, after a life well lived.

More relevantly for our purposes, *The Graduate* propelled the careers of Simon & Garfunkel into the stratosphere,

'The Sound of Silence' is used as a repeated motif throughout the film, reflecting Braddock's feelings of emptiness.

no mean feat given that the duo were already a successful entity by '67. It turned out that the three new songs had been commissioned after Nichols had used existing Simon & Garfunkel cuts as placeholders in early cuts of the movie: he soon realised that their emotional but intellectual tones would be perfect for his college love drama, with 'The Sound of Silence' appearing not once but three times in the final movie.

What's interesting, given that 'Mrs Robinson' is so closely associated with *The Graduate*, is that the version that most of us know and love doesn't actually appear in the film. Instead, we hear a strummed, partwork version of the song early in the movie that focuses on the 'dee-dee-dee' lines, followed later by a short rendition of a chorus that quickly tails off.

These two short versions of 'Mrs Robinson' were released on the film's soundtrack LP on 21 January 1968, while the full version appeared on Simon & Garfunkel's *Bookends* album on 3 April, and as a standalone single two days later. The Grammy awards reaped by the song and movie included 'Best Original Score Written for a Motion Picture or Television Special', shared between Simon and composer Dave Grusin for the *Graduate* soundtrack; 'Record of the Year' for 'Mrs Robinson'; and 'Best Contemporary Pop Performance, Vocal Duo or Group' for Simon & Garfunkel themselves.

The Graduate stars Dustin Hoffman as the titular character, Benjamin Braddock, and Anne Bancroft as Mrs Robinson.

The Graduate soundtrack

'Mrs Robinson' remains one of Simon & Garfunkel's best-known songs.

'Mrs Robinson' is now part of the cultural fabric of American music, and has attracted its own lore – such as the tale of a meeting between Simon and the famous baseball player Joe DiMaggio, who is mentioned in the song. Coming face to face with the songwriter at a New York City restaurant in the Seventies, the great sportsman said: "What I don't understand is why you ask where I've gone [in the lyrics]. I just did a Mr Coffee commercial, I'm a spokesman for the Bowery Savings Bank, and I haven't gone anywhere!"

> ❝ The version of 'Mrs Robinson' that most of us know and love doesn't actually appear in the film

Recalling the encounter, Simon explained that, "I said that I didn't mean the lines literally, that I thought of him as an American hero and that genuine heroes were in short supply. He accepted the explanation and thanked me. We shook hands and said good night'. Simon went on to perform 'Mrs Robinson' at Yankee Stadium in DiMaggio's honour when he died in 1999.

You could reasonably state that 'Mrs Robinson' is Simon & Garfunkel's best-known song to this day – apart from perhaps the other major contenders of 'The Sound of Silence' and possibly 'Bridge Over Troubled Water'. What do *you* think?

Discography

BOOKENDS

3 April 1968
Words by Neil Crossley

Released amid turbulent times, this fourth long player was a stunningly daring work and the duo's first classic album

Bookends Theme
Simon & Garfunkel were established stars by the time they began work on their fourth album, but *Bookends* cemented their reputation and placed them in the same league as Bob Dylan, The Beatles and The Stones. It charted at No.1 on both sides of the Atlantic, and at the same time positioned them at the forefront of the counterculture movement. At its heart, *Bookends* is a concept album, which examines a life journey from infanthood to old age. The record opens with this laconic instrumental on a sole acoustic guitar, setting a mystic, peaceful and reflective tone that would resonate across the album.

Save the Life of My Child
On 14 December 1967, Paul and Art entered Columbia Studio A on Seventh Avenue to record this track, whose narrative charts a dramatic tale involving drugs, violence and a mother and child relationship. Paul Simon suffered writer's block on the album and this track and three others were crafted alongside producer John Simon, whose influence can be felt here. A squelching, distorted analogue synth bass ushers in the song and is played on a Moog synthesiser by Robert Moog himself. There are shades of Dylan at his snarling best in Simon's opening scattergun vocal lines. It's a brazen sonic adventure that sounds light years ahead of its time, segueing into something akin to a prog stomp, yet with a strong melodic hook on the chorus.

America
A sonic road trip filled with optimism

Performing on *The Fred Astaire Show* in July 1968.

Bookends

Bookends was a concept album exploring life, aging and mortality.

A lilting soprano saxophone brings an airy, meandering feel to the middle eight section. It's a timeless classic and one of the most popular compositions within the duo's back catalogue.

Overs

One of the four songs created with the help of producer John Simon and recorded in Columbia's Studio A on 16 October 1967. It's a quiet acoustic number about a man preparing to tell his partner that their relationship is over. The track is slow and intimate, delivered almost as a lounge song. Simon brings his performance down to a hush, holding the listener's attention and in the same instant, elevating the emotional intensity of the song. Noticeably, there is no rhyme to the lyrics here, which only adds to its potency: "Why don't we stop foolin' ourselves? / The game is over, over, over / No good times, no bad times / There's no times at all / Just *The New York Times* / Sittin' on the windowsill / Near the flowers."

Voices of Old People

Not a song but a sound collage, recorded on tape by Garfunkel at the United Home for Aged Hebrews in New Rochelle, New York and the California Home for the Aged at Reseda, Los Angeles. This piece reinforces the 'life journey' concept of the album and these audio recordings feature elderly people musing on treasured photographs, illness and living conditions. Their thoughts are both forthright and deeply poignant,

Old Friends

'Old Friends' delves deeper into the album's core concept, focusing on two elderly men sitting on a park bench discussing their lives and their fears about the changes that surround them. Swells of gentle acoustic guitar and strings intro the track, establishing a calming, reflective feel: "Old friends / Sat on their park bench like bookends", begins Simon as a deep, bowed cello enters the mix. Every nuance and texture of the duo's voices is optimised to the full, with close mic-ing enhancing the natural warmth of their respective

and wonder, and one that charts the adventures of two lovers seeking out the real America. The song was inspired by a five-day road trip that Simon and his then-girlfriend Kathy Chitty made in September 1964: "'Kathy' I said as we boarded a Greyhound in Pittsburgh / 'Michigan seems like a dream to me now' / It took me four days to hitchhike from Saginaw / I've gone to look for America." There's a cinematic sweep to the track. As writer Marc Elliot put it in his 2010 biography *Paul Simon: A Life*, the song "tells of the singer's search for a literal and physical America that seems to have disappeared, along with the country's beauty and ideals". The 6/8 waltz time signature has a real swing to it, courtesy of Hal Blaine on drums, Joe Osborn on bass and Larry Knechtel on pipe organ.

> "Bookends is a concept album, examining a life journey from infanthood to old age"

Discography

Critics still debate whether *Bookends* or *Bridge Over Troubled Water* is the pair's best album.

> "'Bookends Theme' is a poignant reflection on a special time long past"

timbres. Here, Garfunkel's otherworldly high tenor really comes to the fore: "Can you imagine us years from today, sharing a park bench quietly? / How terribly strange to be seventy".

Bookends Theme
'Old Friends' flows seamlessly into the second version of 'Bookends Theme', with high strings and introspective lyrics about a past relationship now accompanying the nylon-strung acoustic, played with great feel and restraint by Simon. It's heartbreakingly poignant, a reflection on a special time long past: "Time it was and what a time it was, it was / A time of innocence / A time of confidences / Long ago, it must be / I have a photograph / Preserve your memories / They're all that's left you."

Fakin' It
An infectious loping groove underpins the first track on side two, which largely consists of previously released singles and unused material for *The Graduate* soundtrack. It's a breezy pop track, with an airy, late-60s French pop vibe, complete with handclaps. Lyrically, the song finds Simon pondering his occupation and what his life would have been like if he had been born a century earlier. At 2:17, there's a spoken word couplet from English singer-songwriter Beverley Martyn – "Good morning Mr Leitch / Have you had a busy day?" – a reference to Simon's contemporary, Donovan. For all its charms there are moments where it sounds aimless, a song in search of a defining sound, although it does reflect the times and points towards prog indulgences of the following decade.

Punky's Dilemma
One of two songs that Simon initially offered to director Mike Nichols for his film *The Graduate*, although Nichols was allegedly unimpressed. Created during the midst of Paul Simon's writer's block, this was one that producer John Simon helped to forge. The team reportedly spent over 50 hours honing the track, often recording it note by note. The result is an endearingly minimal and breezy track, with a wry, light swing style, which

Performing on the Smothers Brothers Comedy Hour in October 1967.

focuses on a young man's quandary about whether to resist the Vietnam War draft.

Mrs Robinson
Few Simon & Garfunkel tracks have taken on such iconic status as this one, written specifically for the 1967 film *The Graduate*. After flatly rejecting two earlier Paul Simon compositions, director Mike Nichols heard a few chords of a new song he was working on, provisionally entitled 'Mrs Roosevelt'. Nichols was ecstatic about the song and suggested that Simon change the title to 'Mrs Robinson', the character immortalised in the film by actor Anne Bancroft. "They filled in with 'dee de dee dee de dee dee dee' because there was no verse yet," Nichols told writer Marc Elliot in 2010, "but I liked even that". Released on 5 April 1968, the song became the duo's second single to reach No.1 in the US and the UK. Although it was released more than three months after *The Graduate*, the song's high rotation radio airplay became pivotal to the cross-promotion of the film.

A Hazy Shade of Winter
This track was recorded at the sessions for *Parsley, Sage, Rosemary and Thyme*

and released as a standalone single back in October 1966, reaching No.13 in the *Billboard* Hot 100 chart. There's a more rock-based feel to the song, which zips along with a Stax-style beat at 142bpm. The song dates back to Simon's days in England and is reminiscent of bands such as The Byrds or The Mama & The Papas. Lyrically, it follows a hopeless poet, with "manuscripts of unpublished rhyme", unsure of his achievements in life. Two decades later, The Bangles covered the song for the soundtrack of the film *Less Than Zero*, and it reached No.2 when released as a single in the US.

At the Zoo
One of Simon's numerous tributes to his native New York, 'At the Zoo' was written for *The Graduate* – specifically the scene at San Francisco Zoo – although it was never used in the film's final cut. The song focuses on a trip to Central Park Zoo, with Simon wryly apportioning human virtues and traits to various creatures along the way. It's a carefree, bouncy track, with a kind of childlike innocence, and showcasing the plate reverb sound that would feature in 'The Boxer' on the duo's next album.

Credit: Getty Images. Adobe Stock

Chapter 2

After 1967, Simon & Garfunkel were on top of the world – so why were clouds gathering on the horizon?

WORDS BY **DAVE SMITH**

The Beginning of the End

On a roll from *The Graduate* and its shelfload of awards, and with Paul Simon's writer's block successfully dispelled, Simon & Garfunkel rolled into 1968 with album number four, *Bookends*. Released on 4 April, the LP was shorter and more precisely crafted than their previous albums, thanks to a couple of specific nuances around its creation. One of these was that the duo's contract with Columbia specified that the company had to pay for any session players employed to record – and as a maturing songwriter, Simon took full advantage, arranging parts for viola, brass and percussion.

The use of novel instrumentation – familiar or otherwise to Western ears – was, of course, nothing new for Simon. Back in 1965, he'd heard the Peruvian band Los Incas playing charangos and pan flutes, and borrowed those sounds for the famous Simon & Garfunkel song 'If I Could'. As he explained in an interview with *Rolling Stone* years later, "I'd never heard those instruments. I loved it. Maybe I have the capacity to have my emotions touched by sounds and rhythms of different cultures, as well as the first stuff I heard on the radio

Chapter 2

in adolescence, when most people's emotions are touched."

The new LP was also more of a 'two solo singers' affair than before, with fewer close harmonies shared between the two men, and Art Garfunkel taking the lead vocal on certain songs. Fans loved this more focused approach, and *Bookends* soon topped the *Billboard* charts. Three of its songs – 'A Hazy Shade of Winter', 'At the Zoo' and 'Fakin' It' – had already been issued as singles, and a new one, 'Mrs Robinson', was for all intents and purposes the song of 1968. A fifth single, 'America', was issued in 1972, although by that time the world of Simon & Garfunkel looked rather different.

Bookends stayed on the US charts for 66 weeks, dipping in and out of the top spot and ultimately scoring seven weeks there. It was anticipated so keenly that it certified gold before copies even left the packaging plant, a rare phenomenon which only takes place when a record's pre-orders are immense.

Columbia took full advantage of this fact, mentioning its pre-order status in industry advertising, and indeed Clive Davis suggested that the album be sold at a full dollar more than the usual market price: with over 5 million copies eventually shipped, this would have made keen business sense. However, Simon is said to have disliked this rampantly commercial approach, leading to a fallout between him and the Columbia boss.

In the wake of *Bookends*, Simon & Garfunkel were a huge commercial property, with the music industry eating from their collective hands. The movie business was their bosom buddy, too, given the vast success of *The Graduate*: it's ironic to note that the film world had made Simon & Garfunkel superstars, but it was also Hollywood that indirectly drove them apart.

Simon turned down the approaches of producers who wanted him to sprinkle some *Graduate*-style songwriting magic on their films, as well as saying no to pitches by directors Franco Zeffirelli and John Schlesinger, who were working on *Brother Sun, Sister Moon* and *Midnight Cowboy* respectively. He also declined a request from the producers of the Broadway show *Jimmy Shine* – even though it starred his *Graduate* chum Dustin Hoffman – and abandoned work on a sacred mass alongside Leonard Bernstein, citing discomfort with this kind of writing.

However, the movie industry is a persuasive animal, and by early 1969 both Paul Simon and Art Garfunkel had signed up to Mike Nichols' World War II film *Catch-22* – not as songwriters, but as actors. Simon took the part of an airman called Dunbar, while Garfunkel played an officer, Captain Nately; however,

The *Songs of America* TV special was surprisingly controversial at the time for its anti-war sentiments.

By the end of the 1960s, Simon & Garfunkel were the world's most famous rock duo.

Garfunkel (centre) played Captain Nately in the 1970 satirical war film, *Catch-22*.

> ❝ Bridge Over Troubled Water spent a staggering 285 weeks in the UK Top 100

The Beginning of the End

The two men did reunite after *Catch-22* wrapped, delivering a series of US and British dates, but it seems with hindsight that the writing was on the wall for them. Their next project – which, on paper at least, should have been another major hit – came in the form of a TV special for the CBS network called *Songs of America*. Directed by Charles Grodin, a well-known actor who had appeared in *Catch-22*, the programme was a montage of scenes dedicated to current and former political figures and key events.

Songs of America depicted the Vietnam War, the funeral procession of JFK, and the life of the late Martin Luther King Jr – who had been murdered just one day after the release of *Bookends* in April 1968 – but it failed to convince the public. CBS were reportedly uncertain about its content, and as a BBC review snidely put it, "one million viewers responded by turning the dial and watching the figure skating on NBC instead."

Still, this minor speed-bump in the commercial progress of Simon & Garfunkel meant little in comparison to the vast impact of *Bridge Over Troubled Water*, released in January 1970 and making it clear once and for all that the duo were a huge creative force with a large and loyal fanbase. As you can read in the album's dedicated entry, Simon's songwriting skills had apparently not been affected by Garfunkel's absence, with several songs from the LP carving a niche as permanent fan favourites.

The statistics bear this claim out: *Bridge Over Troubled Water* made Number One in the album charts in ten countries, becoming the biggest-selling American album of the year not only in 1970 but in '71 and '72 too. It remained in the US charts for 85 weeks, and a staggering 285 weeks – or five and a half years – in the UK Top 100. Over the years it has sold over 25 million copies, and was CBS's biggest LP until Michael Jackson's *Thriller* came along in 1982.

As we'll see, even this huge triumph wasn't enough to keep Simon and Garfunkel together: we'll explore this further in our next chapter. Make no mistake, though: still greater highs – and lower lows – lay ahead.

Bridge Over Troubled Water was the duo's most successful album, but it would be their last.

the former part was written out before filming and only Garfunkel went on to take part.

This is where the seeds of discord were sown between Simon and Garfunkel, it later emerged. With his partner waiting around on a film set in Sonora, Mexico, for most of 1969, it was left to Simon to start work on their next album – an undisputed all-time-classic titled *Bridge Over Troubled Water*.

"We didn't really fight until [that album]," Simon told *Rolling Stone* in 2011. "That had a lot to do with Artie making a movie at the same time."

It turned out that Simon felt abandoned by Garfunkel, although there must have been more to the separation than that: after all, both men had initially signed up to *Catch-22*. Perhaps Simon felt that Garfunkel had betrayed him by going ahead with the film after his own part had been cancelled? Neither man has talked in depth about the reasons for the oncoming schism, however, only referring vaguely to growing apart.

You can read between the lines of *Bridge Over Troubled Water*'s lyrics if you want a view of Simon's thinking at the time. For example, on the song 'The Only Living Boy in New York', a character called Tom flies down to Mexico, leaving the narrator with "nothing to do today but smile."

Credit: Alamy, Getty Images

Discography

BRIDGE OVER TROUBLED WATER

26 January 1970
Words by Neil Crossley

On their fifth and final studio album, Simon & Garfunkel created a masterwork that would become one of the best-selling records of all time

Garfunkel and Simon at the Grammys in 1971, where they picked up three awards including Album of the Year.

Bridge Over Troubled Water

'Bridge Over Troubled Water' is arguably the duo's most famous song.

Bridge Over Troubled Water

This was the song that spearheaded the album, a composition that is as spiritual and soaring as it is moving and sad, and one with a universal theme of hope for the heartbroken and the lost. Simon wrote the song in early 1969 and its lyrics focus on providing comfort to a person in need. "It came so fast," he told Anthony Decurtis of *New York Magazine* in October 2020, "and when it was done, I said, 'Where did that come from? It doesn't seem like me'." Ace LA session band The Wrecking Crew provided the 'Wall of Sound' instrumentation. Simon was adamant that Garfunkel should sing it alone, "the white choirboy way". The song reached No.1 on both sides of the Atlantic. When the duo's relationship became frayed in 1970, Simon began to wish he had sung it himself. "Many times on a stage'" he told author Marc Elliott in 2010, "when I'd be sitting off to the side and Larry Knechtel would be playing the piano and Artie would be singing 'Bridge', people would stomp and cheer when it was over, and I would think, 'That's my song, man'."

El Condor Pasa (If I Could)

There's a calm reassurance running through this delicately textured album, as highlighted on this cover of a Peruvian folk melody written by composer Daniel Alomía Robles in 1913. Paul Simon first heard the song in 1965, while participating in a performance in Paris with the band Los Incas. In 1969, Simon & Garfunkel recorded the Los Incas version, adding English lyrics. Coming after the grandiose conclusion of the title track, this is a beautiful contrast, a sensitive, moving ballad with a pastoral feel. The song was not released as a single in the UK but reached No.1 in Spain, Austria, Australia and Germany.

Cecilia

Released in April 1970 as the third single from the album, this song's origins stemmed from a late-night party at which the duo and their friends began banging with their hands on a piano bench. They recorded the sound on a tape machine, adding reverb to match the rhythms created. Simon then added the guitar line and lyrics about an untrustworthy lover. There's a real energy and warmth to the track, and an appealing rawness from its spontaneous creation. The song was a hit single in the US, peaking at No.4, and it went top five in Canada, Germany, the Netherlands and Spain, although it failed to chart in the UK.

Keep the Customer Satisfied

Released as the B-side of the 'Bridge Over Troubled Water' single, this composition finds Simon seemingly recounting his unease with the gruelling cycle of tours and promotion that he and Garfunkel were locked into. Sonically, it's a light acoustic pop-rock composition, with a shuffle beat and an airiness that belies its lyrical content: "It's the same old story, yeah / Everywhere I go, / I get slandered, libelled / I hear words I never heard in the Bible / And I'm one step ahead of the shoe shine / Two steps away from the county line / Just trying to keep my customers satisfied."

So Long, Frank Lloyd Wright

Bridge Over Troubled Water spans a broad palette – gospel, rock, R&B and classical – a mix of styles and rhythms rarely heard on an album at the juncture of the two decades. This paean to modernist architect Frank Lloyd Wright is a folksy bossa nova with a timeless, laconic feel. Its carefree baroque pop charms are enhanced by congas, strings and flute, while the lyrics evoke the sense of life stages closing. "Architects may come, and architects may go / And never change

> "The title track's universal theme was hope for the heartbroken and the lost

The huge success of *Bridge Over Troubled Water* was not enough to keep the pair together.

your point of view / When I run dry / I'll stop a while and think of you."

The Boxer
Along with 'Bridge Over Troubled Water', this is the second of the album's two big-themed masterworks, becoming a global hit when released as a single in March 1969. 'The Boxer' is one of the duo's most highly produced songs and took over 100 hours to record. Simon's plaintive lyrics reflect on poverty and loneliness. "I think I was reading the Bible around that time," he recalled. "That's where I think phrases such as 'workman's wages' came from, and 'seeking out the poorer quarters'. That was biblical." It's a beautiful top line melody, set against a relatively simple chord structure in the key of C. The "lie, lie, lie" hook was simply the result of Simon being unable to think of words for that section. This refrain is followed by a colossal snare sound, recorded by drummer Hal Blaine, who was set up for maximum sonic effect by producer Roy Halee in the hallway in front of an elevator at the Columbia Records offices. "Roy had me come down on my snare drum as hard as I could," recalled Hal Bliane. "In that hallway, by the elevator shaft, it sounded like a cannon shot! Which was just the kind of sound we were after."

Baby Driver
There's a gritty, unbridled bluegrass feel to this pacey track with its infectious 164 bpm shuffle beat and percussive steel guitar zing. It's fun-soaked and frivolous with more than a nod to the duo's high school rock'n'roll origins: "My daddy was the family bassman / My mamma was an engineer / And I was born one dark grey morn / With music coming in my ears / In my ears".

The Only Living Boy in New York
Paul Simon makes a thinly veiled reference to Art Garfunkel in the first verse of this track, specifically the

Bridge Over Troubled Water

time Garfunkel – referred to here as 'Tom' from their days performing as Tom & Jerry – flew to Mexico to star in the film *Catch-22*, while Simon was in New York writing songs for this album. "Tom, get your plane right on time / I know your part'll go fine / Fly down to Mexico / Doh-n-doh-de-doh-n-doh / And here I am / The only living boy in New York." It's an intoxicating track, with a crisp acoustic feel and a peerless groove from session players Larry Knechtel (Hammond organ), Joe Osborn (bass), Fred Carter Jr (acoustic guitar) and Hal Blaine (drums).

Why Don't You Write Me
A slinky track and the first to find Paul Simon experimenting with reggae although the kick drum is far too firmly on the on-beat to create anything resembling a convincing reggae groove. One minute in and some deep horns enter the mix, evoking the ska music that Simon had first encountered while living in England in 1965. Texturally, it adds interest to the album, but at moments it veers perilously close to oompah music.

> **'The Boxer' took the duo over 100 hours to record**

Bye Bye Love
The blissful close harmony work of The Everly Brothers, which had always inspired the duo, prompted the inclusion of this classic hit. On the first date of their US tour in October 1970, at Ames, Iowa, the rambunctious crowd began clapping spontaneously when the duo launched into this song. Simon & Garfunkel were fascinated by the sound of the song with the massive backbeat clapping and so included the recording of that performance here.

Song for the Asking
Strings and intricately plucked guitar form the backing for this hushed, contemplative track. At just 1:50, it doesn't linger and its calming, reflective tones feel a fitting conclusion to the album. *Bridge Over Troubled Water* would go on to become the best-selling album of the 1970s in the UK, and reached No.1 in ten countries. The album and the title track were perceived by many as a symbol of quiet reassurance following the social and political turbulence of the late 60s and the implosion of the promises offered by the peace and love generation. It's ironic that in the course of creating such a sublime album, the duo's inspirational partnership would end.

Garfunkel in a scene from *Catch-22* with co-stars Alan Arkin and Martin Sheen.

Credit: Alamy, Getty Images, Adobe Stock

Chapter 3

66 THE BREAKUP

72 ART GARFUNKEL

82 PAUL SIMON

The Break Up

The good times couldn't last forever – Simon & Garfunkel went their separate ways in 1970. Here's how the duo imploded…

WORDS BY **JOEL McIVER**

Chapter 3

"One day, Paul Simon called and said he wanted to meet with me at my office," wrote Columbia head Clive Davis in his 2013 autobiography, *The Soundtrack to My Life*. "When he arrived, he got straight to the point. 'Before others find out, I want you to know that I've decided to split with Artie,' he said. 'I don't think we'll be recording together again'."

As a friend of both musicians, Davis was personally saddened by this news – and at the same time, professionally worried about the impact this would have on Columbia, which had suffered some losses in recent times. At the meeting with Simon in the summer of 1970, he tried to persuade his leading artist that he was unlikely to be as successful as a solo artist as he had been as a duo. The effect of this statement was a) to annoy Simon, and b) to make him even more determined to go it alone.

"I understood Paul's frustrations," reasoned Davis, "and his desire to have more control over his music. I simply believed there were ways to satisfy those concerns without breaking up the duo. I also knew how competitive Paul was and how much he valued success. It would be extremely difficult for him to achieve alone anything like the stratosphere he had reached with Simon & Garfunkel."

With all that said, Davis was not surprised to hear that Simon & Garfunkel were splitting – or more accurately, that the former was deserting the latter. He had witnessed the division between the two men growing for a couple of years at this point

So what exactly had brought the duo to this sad stage? To answer that question fully, as the two musicians never really have, requires a list of transgressions on both their parts. No one comes out of this analysis looking good, so be prepared for some mildly depressing reading.

The schism between Simon and Garfunkel goes back as far as 1957, when they were only 16: even though they were a performing couple, Simon signed a solo deal without his buddy. So what, you might think, but Garfunkel apparently took serious umbrage, writing in his 2017 memoir, *What Is It All But Luminous*: "The friendship was shattered for life... I never forget, and I never really forgive."

By the time success came calling, the two men were on different sides of an imbalance of power. Simon, an insecure fellow by nature, was in regular therapy, as he explained in 1984: "Most people look at me and wonder, 'How could that guy be depressed?'... Being short. Not having a voice that you want. Not looking the way you want to look. Having a bad relationship. Some of that is real. And if you start to roll it together, that's what you focus on."

Garfunkel, it seems, was not averse to triggering his partner's anxieties: as Simon recalled in the 2017 biography *Paul Simon: The Life*: "I remember during a photo session Artie said, 'No matter what happens, I'll always be taller than

Garfunkel reportedly felt stifled by Simon's control of the pair's music.

In later interviews, Garfunkel said he thought Simon was an 'idiot' for ending the duo.

Chapter 3

The '71 Grammys was an awkward post-split event; accepting the award for Record of the Year, Garfunkel just said "thank you" while Simon simply nodded.

you'. Did that hurt? I guess it hurt enough for me to remember 60 years later." Elsewhere, Garfunkel is also alleged to have remarked, "Paul won the writer's royalties. I got the girls", which would be enough to irritate anyone.

Make no mistake, though: Simon held the upper hand in this relationship. Their manager Mort Lewis knew this, saying: "They both envied the other's place in the team. Paul often thought the audience saw Artie as the star because he was the featured singer, and some people probably thought Artie even wrote the songs. But Artie knew Paul wrote the songs and thus controlled the future of the pair."

On top of this, Garfunkel's decision to delay the recording of *Bridge Over Troubled Water* by acting in *Catch-22*, and then repeating this trick when he signed up to act in Mike Nichols' next movie *Carnal Knowledge* (1971), was impossible for the ailing relationship to bear. Davis noted that the films took "a terrible toll on Paul and Artie's relationship" not least because Garfunkel was seeking a movie career as a way to avoid feeling belittled by Simon's huge songwriting talent. "Artie made about $75,000 for his role in *Catch-22*, while he made more than $1 million at the time from *Bridge Over Troubled Water*, so he clearly wasn't acting for the money," he noted, both grimly and accurately.

In the end, it was all about differing personalities. Garfunkel summed this up in 2015, when he told the *Telegraph* about an illuminating meeting with George Harrison: "George came up to me at a party once and said 'My Paul [McCartney] is to me what your Paul is to you'. He meant that, psychologically, they had the same effect on us. The Pauls sidelined us. I think George felt suppressed by Paul, and I think that's what he saw with me and my Paul. Here's the truth: McCartney was a helluva music man who gave the band its energy, but he also ran away with a lot of the glory."

It's the perfect analogy. In the case of The Beatles, two alpha songwriters – Lennon and McCartney – battled for dominance, while the other two members resentfully did what they were told. Halve this exactly, and the same situation applied to Simon & Garfunkel, with a supremely talented songwriter who wrote reams of wonderful compositions, faced with a partner who only sang.

Of course, the caveat there is that Art Garfunkel's singing voice is nothing less than miraculous: it's doing him an injustice to describe him as 'just a singer'. As a matter of fact, this may have been a contributor to the duo's split: Simon once revealed his annoyance that fans believed 'Bridge Over Troubled Water' to be a Garfunkel-penned song, simply because he performed its lead vocal.

"I saw that quote, too," sniffed Garfunkel. "But how many songs did I sing upfront and have a real *tour de force* of vocal? Does he resent that I had that one? I find that ungenerous."

Asked whether he would have walked away from Simon & Garfunkel if the decision had been his to make, he added: "It was very strange. Nothing I would have done… it seems very perverse to not enjoy the glory and walk away from it instead. Crazy. What I would have done is take a rest from Paul, because he was getting on my nerves. The jokes had run dry. But a rest of a year was all I needed. I said: 'I'm not married yet. I want to jump on a BMW motorbike and tour round Europe chasing ladies'."

Still, a split was what Simon wanted, and so it came to pass. While he and Garfunkel pondered their next move as musicians – with solo albums issued in 1972 and '73, respectively – they both made the somewhat unusual decision to go into teaching, at least for a while. Simon taught a course in songwriting at New York University, and Garfunkel signed up as a maths teacher at a school called Litchfield Academy in Connecticut. He later revealed that he would sometimes ask his classes a geometry question, only for a student to ask him what The Beatles were like.

Although the duo only remained apart for two years before a short-lived reunion took place, the music world mourned their loss. The sting of the split stayed with Garfunkel for many years: as recently as 2015, he rhetorically asked: "How can you walk away from this lucky place on top of the world, Paul? What's going on with you, you idiot? How could you let that go, jerk?"

Credit: Getty Images

70

Simon became frustrated by Garfunkel's acting work interfering with the production of their records.

Chapter 3

Actor, walker, poet and keen enthusiast of herbal pleasures: the post-Paul Simon life of Art Garfunkel has been quite a ride…

WORDS BY **JOEL McIVER**

Art Garfunkel

Not yet 30 years old, and with no particular place to be, Art Garfunkel was faced with the classic burden of choice as the aftermath of Simon & Garfunkel's split played out. He could sing, he could act, he could teach… but which of these options would be the best one?

It's a question that, on examining Garfunkel's last 50 years, he seems never to have answered. In a sense, he's a creative everyman, with a burning desire to study and enjoy the world, but everymen never really excel at one specific endeavour – and while he's generally made a success of his life, you can't help but sense that he's never quite fulfilled one of many possible potentials.

At first it seemed likely that Garfunkel would make it as an actor. He could clearly do the job, and made a decent fist of his roles in two Mike Nichols films, *Catch-22* (1970) and *Carnal Knowledge* (1971), shot before and during the breakup with Paul Simon. Indeed, his role in the latter snagged him a nomination for Best Supporting Actor at the 1972 Golden Globe Awards.

The role of 'musician turned actor' is a tough one to play, though, and even though Garfunkel's acting was competent, it's uncertain how willing the public and film industry were to accept him as a made-to-measure movie star. At the same time, he had other avenues that he wanted to pursue, one of them being the aforementioned geometry teaching gig at Litchfield Academy in Connecticut. By early '72 his stint in academia was over, though, and once again he was pondering his next move.

It's no surprise that Garfunkel, a lifelong thinker, tried his hand at teaching mathematics; as much or more so than Paul Simon, he inhabits a landscape of the mind. A keen reader despite a childhood almost devoid of books, by his late teens

Chapter 3

Garfunkel with actress Laurie Bird, circa 1979.

> *He struck gold, literally and figuratively, with the single 'I Only Have Eyes for You'*

he was devouring the written word. Much later in life, when he launched a website, Garfunkel included a year-by-year listing of every book he has read since 1968: the list exceeded 1,000 titles a few years back.

In 1972, his forward motion as a solo artist was delayed somewhat by Simon & Garfunkel's first reunion, a benefit show on 14 June for the presidential candidate George McGovern, as well as that year's *Greatest Hits*, the first of a long line of compilations. These spurred him into action as a singer, and he swiftly recorded his first solo album, 1973's *Angel Clare*. Three singles, 'All I Know', 'I Shall Sing' and 'Travelling Boy' were issued, and while they didn't exactly set the charts alight in the era of Led Zeppelin, Pink Floyd and Black Sabbath, they were at least mildly successful.

By now Garfunkel was married to an architect called Linda Grossman, although this only lasted until 1975: there seems to have been little love between the two. What was he looking for? Perhaps a deeper partnership, such as the one he enjoyed with the actress and photographer Laurie Bird, with whom he was attached from spring '74.

A single called 'Second Avenue' did respectably well that year, and Garfunkel recorded his second album, *Breakaway*

On the set of *Carnal Knowledge* (1971) with co-star Jack Nicholson.

(1975) – in retrospect, a curious title as he teamed up once again with his old chum and nemesis Simon on the song 'My Little Town', also a midsized hit. He struck gold, literally and figuratively, with the single 'I Only Have Eyes for You', a cover of a 1934 song by Harry Warren: this got him the Number One slot in the UK, always a loyal market for Garfunkel and his former colleague.

The times they were a-changing as the Seventies hit its midpoint, and Garfunkel's guest slots with artists such as Stephen Bishop, James Taylor and JD Souther in 1976 were his last truly commercial ventures before the music world imploded. Releasing his third album, *Watermark*, in late 1977, Garfunkel would presumably have watched in dismay as the Sex Pistols, the Ramones, The Clash and hundreds of other gobbing, puking, resolutely non-close-harmony-singing punk bands crawled out of the gutter and into the charts.

1977 was the perfect year *not* to release an Art Garfunkel album, given the

Simon may have been the major creative force, but it was Garfunkel's heavenly vocals and harmonies that brought the duo's songs to life.

Chapter 3

fashions of the day, and so *Watermark* pretty much vanished without a trace. Its lead single, 'Crying in My Sleep', didn't even touch the US Top 40, and he was obliged to throw it a lifeline by recording a vocally impressive but critically weak cover of Sam Cooke's '(What a) Wonderful World'. The ploy was a success, partly thanks to the backing vocalists Paul Simon and James Taylor, and *Watermark* was reissued in 1978 to a rather better reception.

Still, market conditions remained fairly difficult for folk singers from the Sixties as the decade came to a close – Paul Simon wasn't exactly tearing up the airwaves either, it should be noted – and there was no saving the 1979 album *Fate for Breakfast*, at least in America. Despite the release of the singles 'In a Little While (I'll Be on My Way)' and 'Since I Don't Have You', the LP failed to gain traction in Garfunkel's home country.

In a surreal twist, a bunch of errant rabbits gave Garfunkel's career a renewed boost in a single market – the good old UK – when one of its songs, 'Bright Eyes', was released. The high point of his solo catalogue, in much the same way that 'You Can Call Me Al' is the highlight of Simon's, this affecting ballad was also the main theme of the 1978 animated film *Watership Down*. That rare thing, an animation that deeply affected – and in many cases traumatised – adults and children alike, the film was based on a Richard Adams novel about the fate of a warren of talking rabbits. Its scenes of bunny bloodshed and the characters' spiritual relationship with a spooky rabbit-god were more powerful than they sound on paper, and Garfunkel's song was the perfect accompaniment.

His personal life took a sad downturn at this point, when Laurie Bird died by suicide in their Manhattan residence in June 1979. Her death left him in a deep depression, he later acknowledged. He kept himself busy, though, on singing and acting fronts: in 1980 he played a psychiatrist in Nicolas Roeg's *Bad Timing* and sang on a song by Crosby, Stills, Nash & Young, perhaps Simon & Garfunkel's closest allies in the world of folk-rock close-harmony singing.

Garfunkel and Laurie Bird were in a relationship for five years until her tragic death by suicide in 1979.

His own LP, *Scissors Cut*, came out in 1981 and fared no better than any of its recent predecessors, although a fortuitous reunion tour with Paul Simon pulled him out of the commercial doldrums. Garfunkel also moved into writing poetry on that tour: although it sounds like something out of a Bob Dylan song, he was riding a motorbike through rural Switzerland when the muse struck.

Unfortunately, the new alliance with Simon was even more fraught than on previous occasions, despite the success of the Concert in Central Park on 19 September 1981 and the subsequent live release. A new studio album from the duo was reportedly set to appear, but Simon turned it into his next solo LP, *Hearts and Bones*. So much for 'old friends'.

Garfunkel's way of dealing with this and other early-Eighties traumas was to get his boots on and walk, just as Forrest Gump did a decade later. In the early part of the decade he strolled across Japan, taking a number of weeks to do so; he embarked on a more ambitious jaunt in ensuing years by walking across the United States in 40 separate stages, covering the route from New York City to the Pacific coast of Oregon in piecemeal fashion.

A compilation LP called *The Art Garfunkel Album* was released in the UK, with British fans also welcoming a single called 'Sometimes When I'm Dreaming', but otherwise Garfunkel was taking a break from music – one

While Garfunkel enjoyed some solo hits, he rarely matched Simon & Garfunkel levels of commercial success.

Garfunkel as psychologist Alex Linden in *Bad Timing* (1980).

Posing for a photo with his wife Kim and their son James in 2005.

> **" He continued to release albums in the era of classic-rock appreciation**

Art Garfunkel

Garfunkel's biggest solo hits include a cover of 'I Only Have Eyes for You', and 'Bright Eyes' from the soundtrack to *Watership Down*.

go-go music scene, Garfunkel met former model Kim Cermak: they struck up a relationship and were married in 1988. The couple have two sons, Beau and James, the latter of whom is a singer who has toured with his father, as well as releasing music under the stage name Art Garfunkel Jr. The senior Garfunkel came out of his musical retirement in '88 with an album called *Lefty* and three singles, 'So Much in Love', 'When a Man Loves a Woman' and 'This Is the Moment'.

Garfunkel's poetic muse had been fruitful enough by this point to populate an entire book of poems, published as *Still Water* in 1989. It covered a range of themes, including depression at his bereavements and ponderings on friends such as Paul Simon, and signalled the start of a fairly relaxed Nineties for its author. In 1991 he sang the theme for a TV series called *Brooklyn Bridge*, and took on another acting role in the surreal thriller *Boxing Helena* two years later. A live album called *Across America* (1996), a role in a cartoon called *Arthur* (1998) and a stroll across Europe (also '98) took Garfunkel up to the millennium.

He continued to release albums in the era of classic-rock appreciation, with *Everything Waits to Be Noticed* in 2003 and a covers LP called *Some Enchanted Evening* in '06. A couple of busts for weed possession in 2004 and 2005 kept him in the headlines, but what really kept the name 'Garfunkel' on people's lips was a guest appearance in 2009 at a Paul Simon exacerbated by the death of his father, Jacob, in 1986.

As before, Garfunkel came back to creative endeavours after a time: it seemed that these were coping methods for him, as well as a necessary outlet for his talents. These were medium-sized projects at best, but well-received on the whole: he played a part on a concept album called *The Hunting of the Snark* by the 'Bright Eyes' composer Mike Batt in 1986, and appeared the same year in a movie called *Good to Go* as a journalist who is framed for murder.

On the set of the film, a Washington DC-set homage to that city's homegrown

Pictured with his *Boxing Helena* (1993) co-star, Julian Sands.

Chapter 3

Performing 'God Bless America' at a baseball game in June 2014.

show, followed by a full-on Simon & Garfunkel tour the same year.

Just as Garfunkel's career had been resurrected by a bunch of rabbits three decades before, in 2010 it was almost permanently stalled by an errant crustacean. Shortly before Simon & Garfunkel announced a 13-date tour, he choked on a piece of lobster, damaging his vocal chords rather severely.

"At the end of January I did a show in Nicaragua," he told *Rolling Stone*. "I brought my son. We did what you call a 'private'. That means they pay you well so you do a show at Mr Gomez's poolside. The show was great and everything seemed fine. I hit the high notes on 'Bridge' real good… I came home and a few days later I went to the Palm restaurant, where they have great lobsters. I was with my son and I choked on one of the larger strands of lobster. That can send you into a near-panic state if it's bad enough. All seemed to be okay, but a couple of days later I started to find that the swallowing muscle was numb. For the rest of the week I was speaking real hoarse and I couldn't quite swallow properly."

He added: "When I went to a doctor, they put a snake down my throat with a camera to check things out. They said, 'Yeah, one of your two vocal cords is stiffer and fatter than the other one'… As the weeks ensued, I saw that I couldn't finesse my singing in the midrange. I could do the high notes and the low notes. High notes are my stock in trade, thank God. But I couldn't sing, 'When you're weary, feeling small'. I couldn't do anything in the middle where you need that finesse. It's indescribable. I was crude instead of fine."

Despite a well-received version of 'Mrs Robinson' on 10 June at an award ceremony for Mike Nichols, the duo cancelled their tour dates, Garfunkel's pipes not having fully recovered. He promised to return to the stage in 2011, and again in 2012, but without success: in 2013 he said that he was making progress towards being able to sing properly again. Still, at the time of writing, that appears not to be the case: he spent some years working on an autobiography called *What Is It All but Luminous: Notes from an Underground Man* (2017) and in spring 2023 announced that he would not be touring "for the foreseeable future".

Art Garfunkel is in his eighties as we write these words, and still a man with enormous creative talents. Is he finally done with acting and singing? Maybe. Has he ever found the answer to the question, "What do I do after Simon & Garfunkel?" We will never know.

On stage with his son, James, in June 2015. James has adopted the stage name Art Garfunkel Jr.

At the SiriusXM Studios in October 2017 to promote his autobiography, *What Is It All But Luminous*.

Chapter 3

The life and times of the songwriter of his generation, with all the highs and lows that the term implies…

WORDS BY JOEL McIVER

Paul Simon

"You can teach somebody about writing songs. You can't teach someone *how* to write a song, I don't think," mused Paul Simon in 1970, pondering the songwriting course that he taught at New York University that year.

This remark seems to have held true across the half-century-long career that Simon has enjoyed since he called time on Simon & Garfunkel's first partnership: while some of his songs have been phenomenally successful and others have missed the mark, in all cases he has written from native instinct. It's an uncanny creative ability that led his second wife, the late Carrie 'Princess Leia' Fisher, to observe: "If you can get Paul Simon to write a song about you, do it. Because he is so brilliant at it."

Like his estranged partner Art Garfunkel, teaching seems to have been a natural home for Simon, at least in the initial period after their split. He extended this as far as mentoring young musicians; in 1970, he held auditions for a songwriters' workshop, from which six teenagers were chosen. He took them to Columbia Studios, where Bob Dylan happened to be recording his album

Chapter 3

Pictured with his first son, Harper, who was born in September 1972.

Self-Portrait, including a cover of Simon's 'The Boxer'. One of these kids, Melissa Manchester, later became successful and wrote a song in gratitude called 'Ode to Paul'.

Although Simon left formal education shortly afterwards, he and his younger brother, Eddie, co-founded the Guitar Study Center in the early Seventies, later part of the New School institution. He would probably have been too busy to get deeply involved, we can reasonably speculate, as he and his new wife Peggy Harper had a baby son, Harper, in 1972, and his self-titled debut album was out – a highlight of which was the Jamaican music-inspired song 'Mother and Child Reunion', which helped the album hit the Top Five in the US and UK.

In the same busy year, Simon and Garfunkel reunited briefly at the former's appearance at the Cleveland Arena in April. The event was a benefit concert for George McGovern's 1972 presidential campaign – and although McGovern failed to unseat the sitting President, Richard Nixon, at least Simon & Garfunkel fans had witnessed their idols working together on an amicable basis. The future looked bright, at least initially in that respect, as Simon played some guitar parts on Garfunkel's 1973 album *Angel Clare*, contributing backing vocals to the song 'Down in the Willow Garden'.

The reality was that the two singers rarely spoke over the next few years; they would cross paths on the musicians' circuit, and talk business from time to time, but theirs was a professional rather than personal relationship at this stage. Simon in particular was too busy to worry much about this, issuing a stream of music for the rest of the Seventies. His next album, the winsomely titled *There Goes Rhymin' Simon*, was released in 1973 along with the singles 'Kodachrome' and 'Loves Me Like a Rock', all of which were successes. A live album, *Live Rhymin'* (1974), kept Simon's profile high.

In retrospect, it's fair to assess Paul Simon's career as having three high points: the Simon & Garfunkel years, the mid- to late Seventies that we're currently discussing, and of course his enormous, and unexpected, hit of 1986. However, his most consistent decade was definitely the Seventies: when *Still Crazy After All These Years* was released in 1975, the music may have been a little darker thanks to his divorce, but the public and critics still loved it. A single by Art Garfunkel, but written by Simon, called 'My Little Town' was another hit in '75, as was 'Gone at Last', Simon's duet with the singer Phoebe Snow; the man was unstoppable at the decade's midpoint.

At this point, Simon's face began to be seen even more regularly on TV, thanks to the prime-time comedy show *Saturday Night Live*. He was close friends with the show's creator Lorne Michaels, a New York City neighbour of his, and eventually

On the set of *SNL* with long-time friend Lorne Michaels (centre) and George Harrison.

84

Between 1976-78, Simon was in a relationship with actress Shelley Duvall.

Simon and Carrie Fisher pictured on their wedding day in August 1983.

appeared on *SNL* no fewer than 14 times. He hosted its second episode on 18 October 1975, and famously appeared in a turkey outfit in its Thanksgiving episode on 20 November 1976. The clip, in which he yells at Michaels for the supposedly embarrassing outfit, is well worth searching out on YouTube.

Simon ramped up his activities as the Seventies progressed, assembling a benefit show for the New York Public Library, writing music for the

> **" 1986 and '87 were the Years of Paul Simon**

film *Shampoo*, acting in Woody Allen's film *Annie Hall* and releasing a hit single called 'Slip Slidin' Away' and a best-of LP, *Greatest Hits, Etc.*, all by the end of 1977.

By then, the era of punk-rock and disco had arrived, and music fans were becoming more hard-hearted and cynical in their choices – and the early Eighties were tougher terrain for this Sixties and Seventies hero. He did a decent job of acting in 1980's *One-Trick Pony*, and composed its soundtrack, but on release it failed to make a serious impact. As you can read elsewhere, a 1981 reunion with Garfunkel paid the bills, but when Simon returned to his solo career in '83 with an album titled *Hearts and Bones*, it was his lowest seller to date.

Still, better things were afoot. After a two-year relationship with the actress Shelley '*The Shining*' Duvall, Simon struck up a romance with Duvall's chum Carrie Fisher, who he married in 1983. The marriage only lasted a year, but the relationship resumed afterwards and the couple remained an item for several more years. In 1985 Simon sang on USA for Africa's saccharine but useful 'We Are the World', and the prestigious Berklee College of Music awarded him an Honorary Doctor of Music degree in '86, so he had little to complain about.

In any case, 1986 and '87 were the Years of Paul Simon, in effect, thanks to the immense success of *Graceland*, the album that he recorded in South Africa with local musicians. Of this planet-sized LP, we'll just say here that very few artists have achieved a comeback on such a scale, let alone 16 years after their first flush of success. The album sold 16 million copies worldwide and scored the 1987 Grammy award for Album of the Year, elevating its maker to the highest commercial status of his career, before or since.

The question then, of course, was whether Simon could maintain this level of success into the Nineties, a slightly more forgiving decade than the Eighties, in which successful popular music was a little more grown-up. He gave it his best shot with 1990's Brazilian-flavoured

A scene from *One-Trick Pony* (1980), written by and starring Simon.

The song 'Hearts and Bones' was written about Simon's relationship with Fisher.

Simon pictured with the South African choral group Ladysmith Black Mambazo, who he worked with on *Graceland*, in 1987.

Paul Simon

Graceland is widely regarded as one of the best albums of all time.

Simon at the Grammys in 1987, where *Graceland* was awarded Album of the Year.

The Rhythm of the Saints, which did well by anyone's usual standards – but not in the same league as *Graceland*, to which it was inevitably compared.

In 1990, Simon & Garfunkel were inducted into the Rock & Roll Hall of Fame, and the following year the former organised a truly giant event: a concert in New York's Central Park, featuring African and South American bands and pulling in 750,000 fans, a mind-boggling number. He later described the concert – as well as the Born at the Right Time Tour, the live album and an Emmy-winning TV special that accompanied it – as "the most memorable moment in my career".

He was right, too. Commercially speaking, the last 32 years of Paul Simon's career have been a long, steady decline from the giddy high point of those two 1986 and 1990 albums. His work has always been loyally received and his talents have never been in question, but he was then (and is now) a classic artist, a star from a former generation, someone to be cherished but not regarded as a particularly current or challenging force. This is the fate of all successful musicians, who are rarely thought to be as potent as they were at a given high point in the past.

Still, it's a nice problem to have, and Simon continued along his merry way, creating music and touring regularly. A 1992 appearance on *MTV Unplugged* introduced him to the grunge generation, and he married the singer Edie Brickell on 30 May that year. The couple went on to have three children, Adrian, Lulu and Gabriel. His pace slowed down a little in the Nineties as he entered his fifties, although a 1993 reunion with Garfunkel and a three-CD compilation called *Paul Simon 1964/1993* kept him on his toes.

Much of the decade was taken up with Simon's only dodgy creative outing, a musical called *The Capeman*. Now, the production has its fans, many of whom have gone to see it on several occasions. It's a dramatic tale that Simon described as "a New York Puerto Rican story based on events that happened in 1959", focusing on a real-life murderer, Salvador Agron, who wore a cape while offing his victims, before becoming a writer in prison.

Simon worked on the play for a few years before it opened in January 1998, and released an album of songs from the show the year before, but it didn't chart and the play itself tanked, losing $11 million in a single year. People just didn't like it, it seems, and once again Paul Simon's career was at something of a low.

A solution might have been to connect with Garfunkel yet again, but instead Simon chose the next best option and went on a co-headline tour with Bob Dylan in 1999. The show featured both Sixties icons separately and together,

Chapter 3

Simon married fellow singer-songwriter Edie Brickell in May 1992.

and was a marketing exec's dream, with the perfect demographic of fans for both Simon and Dylan lining up to buy tickets. A new album, *You're the One*, was released in late 2000 and capitalised neatly on this newfound success, leading to a major tour.

After the September 11 attacks, Simon was among a group of older American musicians to whom the public looked for reassurance, and this came when he sang 'Bridge Over Troubled Water' on *America: A Tribute to Heroes*, a multi-network benefit, and 'The Boxer' on *Saturday Night Live*. These helped to re-establish him in the wider public consciousness, his catalogue of work now understood as a significant cultural asset, and the music industry rewarded him with an Oscar nomination in 2002 for the theme that he wrote for a family film, *The Wild Thornberrys Movie*.

Further recognition came to Simon & Garfunkel with a Grammy Lifetime Achievement Award in 2003, which they followed up with a world tour the following year: this wound up with a free concert in Rome attended by a staggering 600,000 people. Two years later, the duo sang 'Mrs Robinson' and 'Homeward Bound' at the Concert for New Orleans in aid of Hurricane Katrina victims.

Simon's 2006 album with Brian Eno, *Surprise*, may not have broken open any new territory for him, and awards from the Library of Congress and the Brooklyn Academy of Music in '07 and '08 may not have meant much to this most recognised of musicians, but his commercial stature was unaffected. A 2009 reunion with Garfunkel could not be completed, as you'll read elsewhere, but a 2011 album called *So Beautiful or So What* was celebrated with another major tour, which is really the point.

The position of lauded, awarded elder statesman playing his older hits is one that Simon has occupied since then. A successful co-headline tour with Sting took him from 2013 to 2015, and after a 13th LP of new songs called *Stranger to Stranger*, he effectively went into retirement.

"Showbiz doesn't hold any interest for me," he said in 2018, adding "I am going to see what happens if I let go." A last run of live dates was completed before the pandemic, and – apart from studio projects such as *In the Blue Light*, a set of re-recorded songs – Simon has been only sporadically active since then. He sold his music publishing catalogue to Sony in 2021, and why not? The deal netted him $250 million.

Just before this publication went to press, the 81-year-old Simon announced that he had lost most of the hearing in his left ear. However, this hasn't stopped him producing his 15th solo album, *Seven Psalms*, in May 2023. The record is a sequence of seven tracks, designed to be listened to in its entirety as an unbroken 33-minute suite. It would appear that Simon's story isn't quite over yet.

Performing at the *America: A Tribute to Heroes* fundraising event in the wake of September 11.

In 2022, the Recording Academy hosted a special tribute – *Homeward Bound: A Grammy Tribute To Paul Simon*.

Chapter 4

94
REUNITE, SPLIT, REPEAT

104
SIMON & GARFUNKEL'S LEGACY

First, Paul Simon and Art Garfunkel split up. Then they got back together. Then they split up again… Why can't they just get along?

WORDS BY **JOEL McIVER**

Reunite, Split, Repeat

"We are indescribable. You'll never capture it. It's an ingrown, deep friendship. Yes, there is deep love in there. But there's also shit," sighed Art Garfunkel in an interview with *Rolling Stone* in 2001. Judging by the on-off relationship that the two musicians have endured over the last 50 years, he was right: theirs is a complex part-friendship, part-enmity that will apparently never be resolved.

Consider the evidence. Bands split up and reunite all the time nowadays, of course, and the cause – in both directions – is always money, and nothing else. When Simon and Garfunkel first went their separate ways in 1970, however, we can reasonably speculate that it was nothing to do with money: it was because they annoyed the hell out of each other.

The problem there, of course, is that tempers cool over time and people remember why it was they were friends in the first place. That's when reunions are suggested, and everyone is all chummy again – until people start to get on each other's nerves, yet again, ad infinitum. That's basically why Simon and Garfunkel could never make a reunion last.

They gave it their best shot, though: you have to give them that. Two years after Simon made the fateful call to Clive Davis to confirm the split, he received a call from the actor Warren Beatty. Keen to boost the campaign coffers of George McGovern, the Democratic presidential candidate who planned to take on President Richard Nixon in the 1972 election, Beatty persuaded Simon to take part in a fundraising gig at New York's Madison Square Garden in June that year. Garfunkel was asked if he would appear alongside Simon, and when both men agreed, Beatty realised that he had

Chapter 4

achieved McGovern's slogan promise of 'bringing people back together'.

Around 20,000 people gathered at MSG on 14 June to witness this historic reunion, as well as that of the comedy duo Nichols and May, and the folk group Peter, Paul and Mary. Dionne Warwick also performed and a team of celebs made speeches, as did McGovern himself. From this many years' distance it might seem odd that so much effort would be put into a simple fundraiser, which raised $400,000 (equivalent to about $3 million dollars today). The answer is that Nixon was much hated for essentially running the Vietnam War at the time, a brutal conflict that inflicted a huge death toll on both sides for dubious reasons, in other words the American establishment's fear of communism.

Paul Simon wasn't keen on McGovern but he couldn't stand Nixon, telling *Rolling Stone*: "I do believe in the lesser of two evils, and in that spirit I became a McGovern supporter." He and Garfunkel played eight songs at the show, kicking off with 'Mrs Robinson' and winding up with 'Bridge Over Troubled Water', said to be a favourite of McGovern's. Not for the first

> **A full-on reunion was still some years away**

time, Garfunkel's voice was playing up, obliging Simon to sing the second verse of the song for the first time.

The four hundred grand which McGovern's team pocketed after the show proved to be useless, as he was easily defeated by 'Tricky Dicky' Nixon, with his majority of the American electorate evidently content to continue dropping napalm on the Vietnamese jungle. Still, Simon and Garfunkel had established a precedent, and went back to their solo careers with the idea in mind that perhaps more collaborations might occur between them.

A full-on reunion was still some years away, but between their other commitments the duo worked together on and off in 1975. They came up with a song called 'My Little Town' that both musicians included on solo albums the same year, and they also sang together on *Saturday Night Live*. Two years later they performed together on a self-explanatorily titled TV show called *The Paul Simon Special*, and in '78, Simon joined Garfunkel on stage during a concert held at Carnegie Hall to raise funds for hearing research.

The pair's first post-split performance was at a benefit concert for the Democratic presidential candidate George McGovern, in June 1972.

Reunions

Garfunkel joined Simon for a set when the latter was hosting *Saturday Night Live* in 1975.

Simon & Garfunkel performed at the inaugural BRIT Awards in October 1977.

The first real reunion, and arguably the peak of Simon and Garfunkel's joint careers, came on 19 September 1981 with The Concert in Central Park, the idea of a concert promoter called Ron Delsener. New York City was suffering from economic and environmental decay at the time – as anyone who lived in or visited the place around this time will remember – and the so-called 'green lung' of Central Park was far from green. Restoration of the park required $3 million that the city did not have to spare, and Delsener's idea was that a free show would help kickstart its rejuvenation.

Between the HBO network and Delsener, it was decided that Simon &

The famous Concert in Central Park raised money to help fund maintenance and redevelopment projects in the park.

Garfunkel would be the best headliners for the show, so it was fortunate that the duo agreed to step up. It had been a decade since their split, in other words the perfect opportunity for a comeback for music fans who hadn't enjoyed the pesky new sounds – specifically heavy metal, disco, hip-hop and punk rock – that had come along since 1970. As local New Yorkers, their presence was thought likely to attract large numbers of city-dwellers, a prediction that proved accurate as over half a million showed up.

The Concert in Central Park was huge, critically, commercially and literally, but that didn't mean that all was tickety-boo behind the scenes. True to form, Simon and Garfunkel managed to fall out over petty logistics, in this case the issue of which man got most stage time. Of course, they could just have agreed to play for the same amount of time, but apparently that would have been too simple: the original idea was that Simon – the greater commercial force – would play for longer. You can imagine how that idea was received.

In the end, both singers agreed to perform together and throw in a solo song here and there, a solution that seemed to work even though they were sick of the sight of each other. Simon later admitted, "The rehearsals were just miserable. Artie and I fought all the time," and Garfunkel overthought it hugely by saying, "It didn't seem right to either of us that Paul should be the opening act for Simon & Garfunkel, and for him to follow Simon & Garfunkel didn't make show-business sense."

Add to the mix the fact that neither of them could agree on the instrumentation of their set, let alone the songs that they would be singing, and it's a miracle that the show ever took place. Still, the live

The pair pictured speaking to the press before the Central Park concert in September 1981.

The Central Park event attracted an estimated 500,000 people – one of the largest concert attendances in history at the time.

Chapter 4

The pair performed together when they were inducted into the Rock & Roll Hall of Fame in 1990.

album which followed went double platinum, paying everyone's bills for the next few years, and HBO broadcast the event for a $1 million fee. The duo even kept it together long enough to execute a world tour through 1982, although it was reported that they rarely spoke to each other along the way.

A new Simon & Garfunkel album was originally due to be recorded after the tour wound up, but Simon changed his mind, supposedly annoyed by his partner's fondness for weed and casual attitude towards learning songs. Instead, Simon used the new songs for his next solo album, 1983's *Hearts and Bones*, which would have been something of a slap in the face for his herbally refreshed colleague.

The next few years were punctuated by general expressions of irritation between the two fellows. In 1985, Garfunkel was irked by Simon's extended employment of the studio engineer Roy Halee on the *Graceland* album when he needed Halee's help with his own project, an LP called *The Animals' Christmas*. In 1990, Simon & Garfunkel were inducted into the Rock & Roll Hall of Fame, an event that started well when Garfunkel made a heartfelt speech, thanking Simon and labelling him "the person who most enriched my life by putting those songs through me".

Rather than return the compliment, Simon sniped: "Arthur and I agree about almost nothing. But it's true, I have enriched his life quite a bit," which you'll agree is a touch unpleasant. No wonder the two men sang three songs and then took off without exchanging a word.

In 2003, the duo embarked on the Old Friends reunion tour.

Despite the success of their Central Park concert and tour in 1982-83, Simon and Garfunkel had no intention of reuniting permanently.

Chapter 4

The following year, Paul Simon set up his own concert in Central Park, duly released as a live LP. It's a little depressing to learn that Garfunkel offered to come along and perform, but Simon turned him down. Still, when 1993 rolled around, all the mutual jabs seemed to have been forgotten when the two toured together through the US and Japan.

Can you predict what happened next? Of course you can. In an authorised biography of Paul Simon written many years later by the duo's business manager Joseph Rascoff, it emerged that the '93 shows had seen Simon and Garfunkel come very close to attacking each other. In the book, Simon was quoted as saying: "During one song, I think it was 'The Boxer', I made a mistake over when to come in, and it threw Artie off for a second. But it was an accident; it wasn't intentional. So later, we're singing 'Feelin' Groovy', and suddenly Art just stops singing at the part that goes 'Life, I love you', and I'm just left there by myself, trying to figure out what to do. I assumed it was another mistake – no big deal."

Apparently not, he continued. "But then at intermission, Art comes up to me and says, 'You tried to make me look like a fool on 'The Boxer',' and I said, 'No, Artie, it was a mistake. Mistakes happen, just like you forgot to sing 'Life, I love you'... That's when he looked me in the eye and said, 'I didn't forget. I just wanted you to see what it feels like to be made a fool of'."

It was at that point that the gloves came off and Rascoff was forced to separate the seething singers. He later predicted that, had a knife been present at the time, only one of them would have walked away. Little wonder that another decade passed before they could bear to tour together again.

In the Nineties, the poor relationship between Simon and Garfunkel became a running joke: it would have surely been a social-media meme had the internet existed at the time. The two men knew this and were sometimes able to laugh about it, with Simon saying at his 2001 induction into the Rock & Roll Hall of Fame as a solo artist: "I regret the ending of our friendship. I hope that someday before we die we will make peace with each other." He then waited a comic moment before adding: "No rush."

Still, what goes around comes around, and in 2003 the two men kept things civil enough to perform a full-scale world tour – essentially their final bow, as we'll see. The Old Friends Tour, as it was ironically titled, ran for 60 dates in the US and 12 more in Europe, winding up with a vast free show at the Colosseum in Rome for an astounding 600,000 people.

Two years later, Simon & Garfunkel performed at a Hurricane Katrina benefit concert at Madison Square Garden, and four years later still, they reunited yet again for shows in 2009 through Asia and Australia. More dates were planned for

Pictured at the 25th Anniversary Rock & Roll Hall of Fame Concert in October 2009.

Reunions

On stage at the New Orleans Jazz & Heritage Festival in April 2010.

The duo's last performance together was at the AFI Lifetime Achievement Award event in June 2010.

"Since 2010, the press have constantly asked them if they'll play together again

2010, but Garfunkel's vocal cords were injured when he choked on a chunk of lobster and those shows were cancelled. That, it seems, was that for Simon & Garfunkel, at least as a performing unit.

Since then the press have constantly asked them if they'll play together again, especially as Garfunkel has recovered from his voice injury. "Will I do another tour with Paul? Well, that's quite doable," he told the *Telegraph* in 2015. "When we get together, with his guitar, it's a delight to both of our ears. A little bubble comes over us and it seems effortless. We blend. So, as far as this half is concerned, I would say, 'Why not, while we're still alive?' But I've been in that same place for decades. This is where I was in 1971."

"It takes two to tango," he told *Rolling Stone* around the same time, adding rather brilliantly: "I don't want to be the blushing bride waiting for Paul Simon to walk down the aisle. If he's too busy to work with me I guess the real answer to your question is, 'I'm too busy to work with him'. I think that's the only answer I can give you for pride's sake. But I will say that word 'Yes' because I left that tour of the Far East in 2009 really happy… It sits there as a potential thrill. I know that audiences all over the world like Simon & Garfunkel. I'm with them. But I don't think Paul Simon's with them."

It seems that it's really down to Paul Simon to make it happen, but at the time of writing he's promoting a new solo album, released in May 2023 – and both men are in their eighties. Time is flying, a fact of which he is regretfully aware. "Truth is, I really do enjoy singing with Artie," he told *Rolling Stone*. "The relationship was repaired during that tour [in 2009]. That tour had a big effect on people. People knew we were close friends who'd had a hurtful rift. We said, 'Life's too short'. And the symbolism kind of struck a lot of other people who'd had similar struggles in their own lives."

"Aside from my compassion for him," he concluded, "I also think how terrible it would be if I couldn't sing with Artie again." Food for thought, gentlemen.

How will the world look back on Simon & Garfunkel in years to come – and what legacy do they leave behind them?

WORDS BY **DAVID SIMS**

Legacy

The numbers don't lie. Over 100 million records sold, seven Grammy awards, not one but two inductions into the Rock & Roll Hall of Fame: Paul Simon and Art Garfunkel have done pretty well out of this music lark, albeit the former rather better than the latter. These men have spent the last 60 years living their very best professional lives.

And it's just as well, because at the time of writing in 2023, both musicians are in their early eighties. Both hale and hearty as far as we know, and – in Simon's case, certainly – with new music to promote, their story isn't over, but it's certainly deep into its third act. In a few years their millions of fans will be looking back at Simon & Garfunkel and asking themselves 'What legacy did Paul and Art leave us?'

Chapter 4

Simon & Garfunkel became one of the biggest acts of the 1960s folk-rock scene.

Columbia Records tried to hike the price of *Bridge Over Troubled Water*, just to make a few bucks? Do you recall Simon's decision to go solo, against all commercial advice, and Garfunkel's slightly weird but ultimately profitable venture into acting? These were and are musicians who took risks in the name of that priceless goal, musical autonomy.

On a related note, look how far Simon & Garfunkel's music evolved across their brief career as a duo: we don't even need to mention Simon's huge success with world music in his later career, but it's there if you need evidence. Even in their short seven years together, the pair moved from a fairly mundane mid-Sixties songwriting position through to ethereal folk before amping up their sound and going into truly anthemic territory.

Yes, we'll give full and everlasting credit to the producer Tom Wilson for signing them and revamping their sound, the latter without their knowledge; in doing so, he handed them a career. However, they would have slipped quickly back into obscurity without Simon's exquisite songwriting, Garfunkel's stunning vocals and the willingness of both men to forge ahead with a new sound.

This leads us to another salient point. The duo weren't rock stars, they didn't look like rock stars and they didn't talk like rock stars. Unusually, they were exactly who they seemed to be, which was educated, bookish fellows from a culturally elite background who loved academia and eschewed excesses. Although Garfunkel may have squired a few groupies and smoked a few joints,

> ❝ **The duo weren't rock stars, they didn't look or talk like rock stars**

Let's try to answer that question. First of all, their catalogue of music stands tall alongside any artist of their era, which we should specify as 1964 to 1970. From those exact years, The Beatles, Bob Dylan and The Rolling Stones outperformed them commercially but not critically; everyone else was in Simon & Garfunkel's shadow, if we're gauging this by sheer excellence in songwriting. Other music behemoths may have outsold them – Elvis Presley before them, Led Zeppelin afterwards – but for that specific seven-year period, Simon & Garfunkel were near the top of a very exclusive shortlist.

We remember them also as artists who directed their own careers, right from the start. Remember their resentment when

Performing at the BBC, circa 1967

Over 50 years since their '71 split, Simon & Garfunkel remain popular in the age of streaming, with 12 million monthly listeners on Spotify alone.

'Bridge Over Troubled Water' has become one of the most covered songs in the history of popular music.

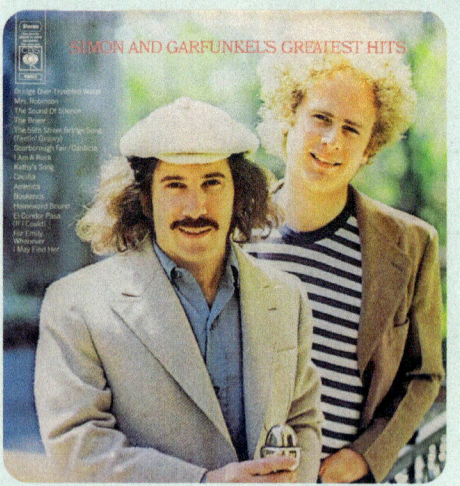

Even after their split, the pair's subsequent compilation records comfortably made the Top 10 in many countries.

Legacy

he hardly lived the life of a sybarite – and as for Simon, he was the straight man's straight man. He even disliked talking about his personal life, telling *Rolling Stone*: "At a certain point, you begin to realise about your life and your private affairs that it's inappropriate that it should be entertainment for somebody else. There's no requirement that I tell how I hurt and how I feel. It's a mistake you make early on."

What other mistakes did Simon & Garfunkel make? Very few, considering their prominence and the longevity of their careers. Neither man was ever cancelled for an inappropriate comment; neither insulted their fans by making an experimental speed metal album. They rarely let people down with undercooked live performances, and they tended not to cancel shows unless ill-health got in the way, although doing so must have been tempting given how badly they annoyed each other on a daily basis. All of that is a lesson for anyone, musician or civilian, who wants to understand how Simon & Garfunkel made things work.

On that note, remember that the duo's classic songs are emotional and sensitive rather than heavy-handed. In their era, with Black Sabbath coming down the line and Jimi Hendrix blowing people's minds with technique and volume, it would have been all too easy to strap on electric guitars and go wild. That was never Simon & Garfunkel's way.

> **Their classic songs are emotional and sensitive**

Like the fable in which the sun's gentle warmth entices a man to remove his coat when the fierce wind can't blow it off him, the duo attracted us to them rather than forcing us to pay attention. Subtlety and sensitivity were the watchwords of their music, a style emulated just after them by James Taylor and other understated singer-songwriters. Listen to any folk band of the last 50 years and, if they sit back in a quiet acoustic groove and speak to your heart rather than to the dancefloor, chances are they've listened to Simon & Garfunkel at some point.

Their songs made people *feel* – and even the cynical old music industry felt something too, judging by the piles of awards its denizens heaped at Simon & Garfunkel's feet over the years. We won't list every gong and statue on Paul and Art's mantelpieces here, but it would be dereliction of duty if we didn't mention at least some of the hardware. The treasure trove begins with Grammy awards in various categories for 'Mrs Robinson' and the *Bridge Over Troubled Water* album in 1969 and 1970, the latter of which scooped no fewer than three awards for Album of the Year, Record of the Year (there's a subtle difference) and Best Arrangement: Accompanying Vocalist(s).

Separately, Garfunkel nabbed a Best Supporting Actor nomination for *Carnal Knowledge* in 1972, and the much more prolific Simon outdid him with several solo Grammys, a Lifetime Achievement

Simon & Garfunkel's 1982-83 world tour drew in many thousands of fans.

Chapter 4

The duo were inducted into the Rock & Roll Hall of Fame in 1990.

Award, and even a Best Original Song Oscar nomination for the song 'Father and Daughter' in 2002. As we mentioned, both men were entered into the Rock & Roll Hall of Fame in 1990, and Simon was inducted as a solo artist in 2001. He has also been awarded MusiCares Person of the Year (2001), Kennedy Center Honors (2002), a BMI Icon (2005), the Library of Congress Gershwin Prize for Popular Song (2007), an honorary degree from Brandeis University in Massachusetts (2010), an induction into the American Academy of Arts and Sciences (2011) and a Polar Music Prize (2012). It clearly pays to write good songs, a fact that Garfunkel has no doubt grimly noted.

Still, considering the idea of what he leaves behind is evidently not a major priority for Simon. As he told Christiane Amanpour of CNN a few years back, "I don't believe in legacy. I don't believe that there's any importance to it. I've already left a great deal of my thinking… through these songs – some of which are very, very well-known – so it's good to stop and see what else I think of. Or maybe I won't. Maybe I'll just take a rest."

He added: "It's not like I couldn't do another album now at the same qualitative level as I've done the last two or three albums – which I think are as good as I can do, as I've ever been. I think I could do that, but I'm not sure that's the most interesting choice for me… [but] I can't help but think music. It seems it's always there. I wake up with it."

Garfunkel is even less interested in his posthumous legacy, scoffing to PBS: "I've heard that word. They like that word a lot these days. I don't know what that means. I have a wife and kids. I have a family. I know what *that* means. What is my legacy? The world and all of its glamorous stars is a hit parade. They come up and then they go down. Except for J S Bach. He seems to stay up there, but I'm discouraged by that. How we love certain people and then it fades. I've heard kids say, 'Sinatra? Who's Sinatra?' They never heard that word. I take this very poorly. I want them to think Simon & Garfunkel had it. They were indelible. We did something that has value through the decades."

The fact is that Simon & Garfunkel's music isn't going anywhere. It has penetrated the cultural fabric on a global level, and not just for folk-music lovers. You may recall the *Popstars* talent-show band Hear'Say covering 'Bridge Over Troubled Water' in 2001; you may also be familiar with the more recent cover of 'The Sound of Silence' by the American metal band Disturbed. Released in 2015, their grandiose cover of the classic song attracted the attention of Paul Simon himself, as well it might given that it sold 1.5 million downloads and was streamed 54 million times.

He wrote to Disturbed singer David Draiman, saying "Really powerful performance on [TV show] *Conan* the other day. First time I'd seen you do it live. Nice. Thanks." The gobsmacked Draiman replied, "Mr Simon, I am honored beyond words. We only hoped to pay homage and honor to the brilliance of one of the greatest songwriters of all time. Your compliment means the world to me/us and we are eternally grateful."

There are dozens of these cover versions, from Aretha Franklin's 1971 take on 'Bridge Over Troubled Water' via the Lemonheads' excellent grunge cover of 'Mrs Robinson' in 1992, through to 'The Boxer' by Emmylou Harris, Neil Diamond, Bruce Hornsby, Bob Dylan and many more. These songs are just too good to go away, it seems – and that is both the legacy that Simon & Garfunkel leave behind, and the gift they have bequeathed us. No one could ask for more.

In 2013, *Sounds of Silence* was added to the Library of Congress' National Recording Registry due to its cultural importance.

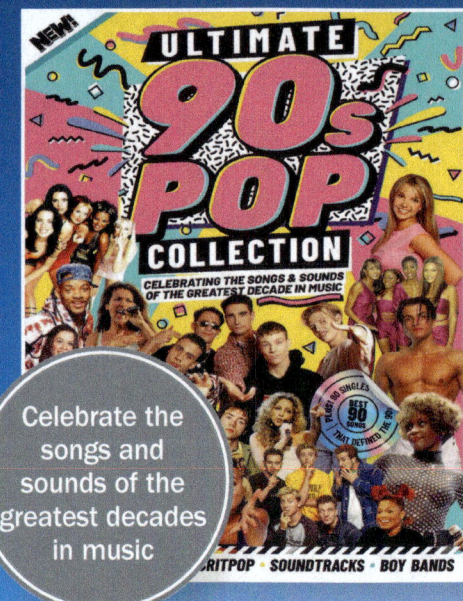
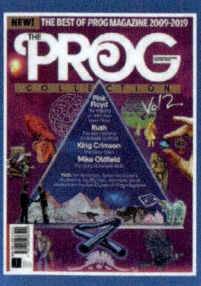
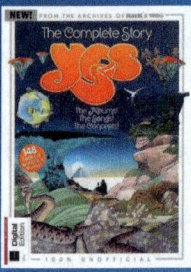
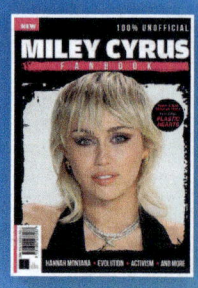
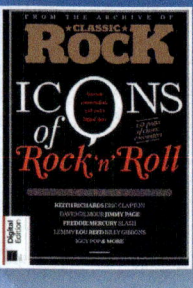

Celebrate the songs and sounds of the greatest decades in music

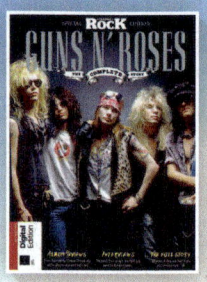

Explore the lives and legacies of some of the world's most iconic artists

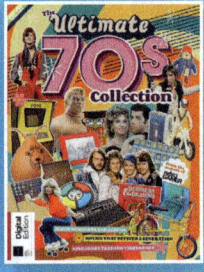

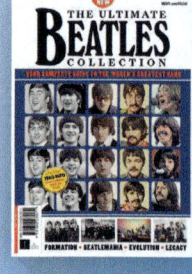
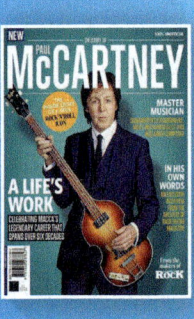
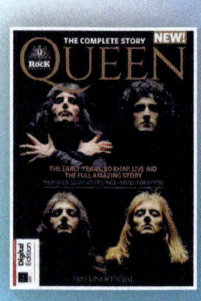
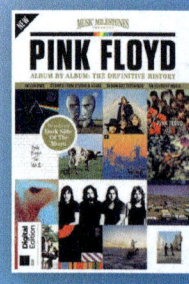

Crank up the volume and get to know the best rock and metal bands on the planet

Get great savings when you buy direct from us

1000s of great titles, many not available anywhere else

World-wide delivery and super-safe ordering

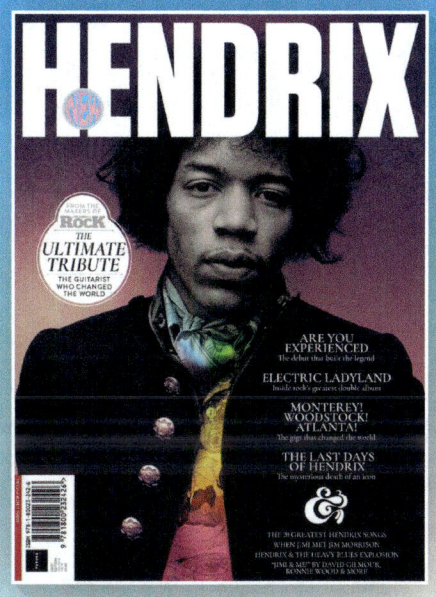
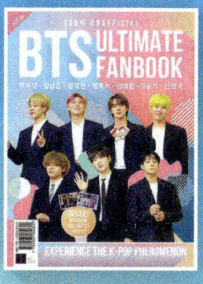

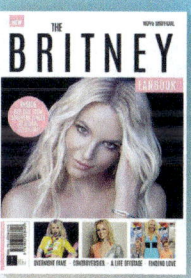
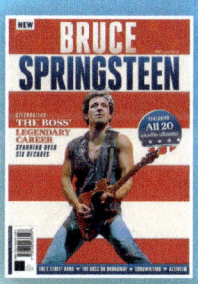

ROCK ON WITH OUR MUSIC BOOKAZINES

Discover the origins of legendary songs, relive iconic performances and meet the pioneers behind some of music's greatest names

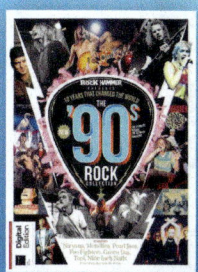
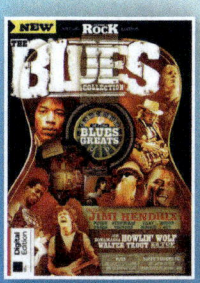

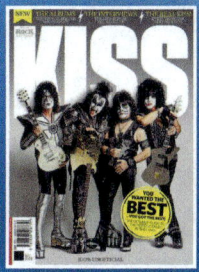
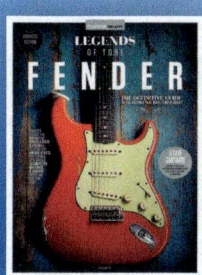

Discover everything there is to know about your favourite pop stars

Follow us on Instagram @futurebookazines

www.magazinesdirect.com
Magazines, back issues & bookazines.

FUTURE

RELIVE THE FASCINATING TALE OF THE ICONIC FLEETWOOD MAC

Explore the incredible story of Fleetwood Mac's journey and evolution from British blues band to soft-rock megastars, revisit each of their 17 studio albums and discover the drama-filled making of their classic 1977 album *Rumours*

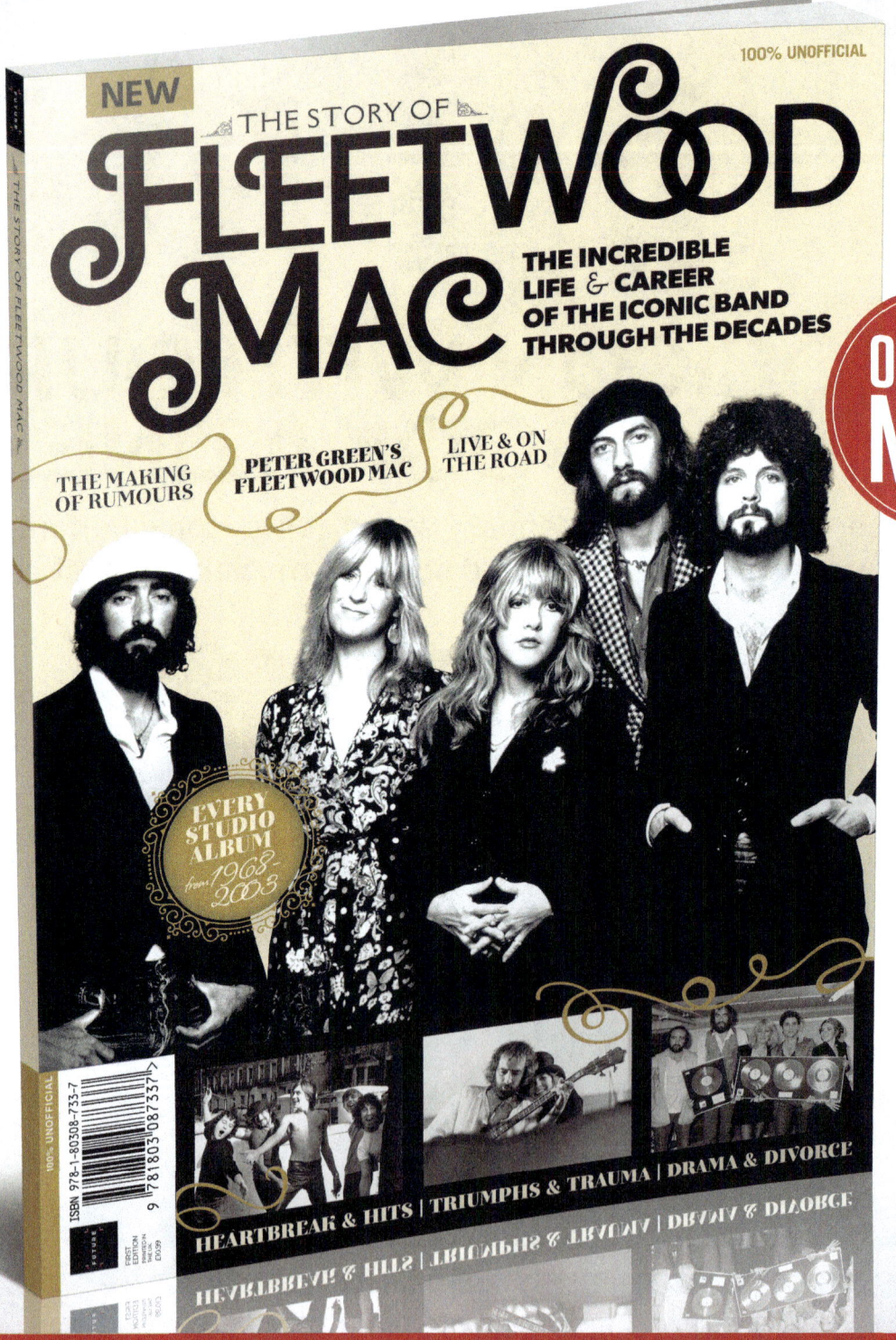

Ordering is easy. Go online at:
magazinesdirect.com
Or get it from selected supermarkets & newsagents

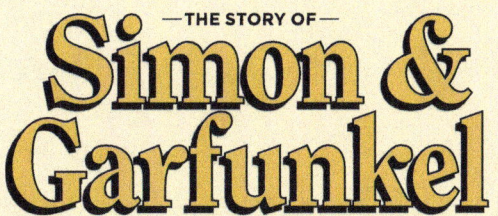

The Story of Simon & Garfunkel

Future PLC Quay House, The Ambury, Bath, BA1 1UA

Editorial
Editor **Jacqueline Snowden**
Senior Designer **Phil Martin**
Head of Art & Design **Greg Whitaker**
Editorial Director **Jon White**
Managing Director **Grainne McKenna**

Contributors
Neil Crossley, Joel McIver, Dan Peel

Cover image
Getty Images

Photography
All copyrights and trademarks are recognised and respected

Advertising
Media packs are available on request
Commercial Director **Clare Dove**

International
Head of Print Licensing **Rachel Shaw**
licensing@futurenet.com
www.futurecontenthub.com

Circulation
Head of Newstrade **Tim Mathers**

Production
Head of Production **Mark Constance**
Production Project Manager **Matthew Eglinton**
Advertising Production Manager **Joanne Crosby**
Digital Editions Controller **Jason Hudson**
Production Managers **Keely Miller, Nola Cokely, Vivienne Calvert, Fran Twentyman**

Printed in the UK

Distributed by Marketforce, 5 Churchill Place, Canary Wharf, London, E14 5HU www.marketforce.co.uk – For enquiries, please email: mfcommunications@futurenet.com

The Story of Simon & Garfunkel First Edition (MUB5312)
© 2023 Future Publishing Limited

We are committed to only using magazine paper which is derived from responsibly managed, certified forestry and chlorine-free manufacture. The paper in this bookazine was sourced and produced from sustainable managed forests, conforming to strict environmental and socioeconomic standards.

All contents © 2023 Future Publishing Limited or published under licence. All rights reserved. No part of this magazine may be used, stored, transmitted or reproduced in any way without the prior written permission of the publisher. Future Publishing Limited (company number 2008885) is registered in England and Wales. Registered office: Quay House, The Ambury, Bath BA1 1UA. All information contained in this publication is for information only and is, as far as we are aware, correct at the time of going to press. Future cannot accept any responsibility for errors or inaccuracies in such information. You are advised to contact manufacturers and retailers directly with regard to the price of products/services referred to in this publication. Apps and websites mentioned in this publication are not under our control. We are not responsible for their contents or any other changes or updates to them. This magazine is fully independent and not affiliated in any way with the companies mentioned herein.

Future plc is a public company quoted on the London Stock Exchange (symbol FUTR)
www.futureplc.com

Chief Executive Officer **Jon Steinberg**
Non-Executive Chairman **Richard Huntingford**
Chief Financial and Strategy Officer **Penny Ladkin-Brand**

Tel +44 (0)1225 442 244

Printed in Dunstable, United Kingdom